WHAT HAPPENS TO CHILDREN
The Origins of Violence

A collection of stories
told by children who could not write them

Edited by

VALERIE YULE

Angus & Robertson Publishers

Author's Note

None of the inner-urban children in the photographs told any of the stories in this book. The pictures have been selected as positive evidence to emphasise the main point of the book—that children are human, sensitive, vulnerable, and can be our greatest joy.

All photographs by F.K. McLennan except those on p. 42 (Oliver Strewe) and p. 84 (John Fairfax & Sons Ltd.)

The stories are given verbatim, apart from changes of names throughout, although ethnic origin is still indicated. Some minor descriptive details have been changed to ensure the children's anonymity.

ANGUS & ROBERTSON PUBLISHERS
London · Sydney · Melbourne · Singapore · Manila

First published by Angus & Robertson Publishers, Australia, 1979

© Valerie Yule 1979

National Library of Australia
Cataloguing-in-publication data.

What happens to children.

Index
ISBN 0 207 13807 9 paperbound
ISBN 0 207 14201 7 hardbound

1. School prose. 2. School verse. 3. Children's writings, Australia.   I. Yule, Valerie, ed.

A820'.8092'375

Filmset in Hong Kong by Asco Trade Typesetting Ltd.
Printed in Hong Kong

WHAT HAPPENS TO CHILDREN

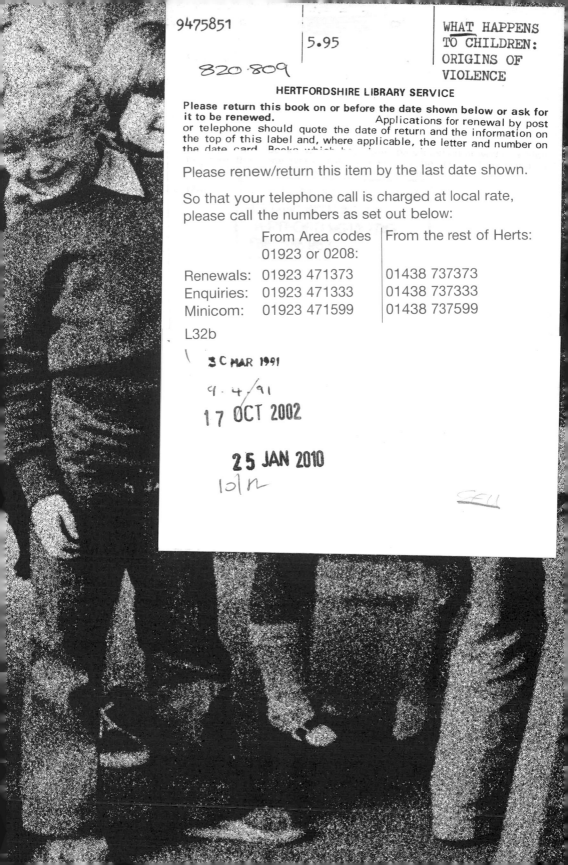

9475851

5.95

820.809

WHAT HAPPENS
TO CHILDREN:
ORIGINS OF
VIOLENCE

Contents

Acknowledgements

I thank the children who have given me permission to show their stories to other people.

I am grateful to all who have made comments on any of the many drafts, particularly Dr Ruth Wertheim, Dr Cliff Judge and Mr John Laffin, and to those who have helped with typing and encouragement —Ms Winsome de Posamentier, Ms Paula Piddington, Ms Beverley Goldsworthy, and my family. Part of the work has been done as one aspect of an Innovations Project, "An Integrated Approach to the Problems of Children with Special Needs", funded by the Australian Schools Commission. This assistance is acknowledged with gratitude, and it is my hope that this book will help to achieve its aims.

VALERIE YULE

Ormond College,
Melbourne,
Australia.

Foreword

I am glad to welcome this new book of stories told by children who could not write them—**What Happens to Children**.

Any of us who aim to help children with their problems know how difficult it can be to assess the family situation as a whole, by means of verbal communication. Indeed, no child psychiatrist would expect to do that. Hence, play, painting, and a free outlet of fantasy, watched, shared, considered and interpreted back to the child is the basic raw material of most treatment sessions.

It needs a comfortable and safe feeling on the part of a child to share with an adult some of the more turbulent and destructive fantasies that are there in his mind. Also we must remember that to use speech, and even more so written language, is to use a relatively late developmental acquisition; but telling them stories is an age-old activity of all those who love and care for children.

Here we are given stories just as they are told *by* the children. It can be a rich, and also a disturbing experience, both to the giver and to the receiver.

With these records in front of us we can begin to reflect on what they meant to the children who used this means to express their own feelings. It is a book to be read and shared by all concerned with basic realities in children's lives. We can be grateful to Valerie Yule for making these stories available.

MILDRED CREAK
formerly Physician to the Department of Psychological Medicine, Hospital for Sick Children, Great Ormond Street, London.

About the Stories

Fifteen years ago I was talking with a boy, and I casually asked him to draw anything he liked, and when he had begun drawing, I asked him if he would tell me a story about the picture when he had finished it. The story was *The ugly duckling* (Story 9, p. 35) which was not only an accurate description of himself at the time, but also accurately foretold that he would grow up to be "a beautiful swan". Since then, talking with nearly two thousand children, I have found how easily they can tell stories about their free drawings in a situation where they feel safe and by themselves, with someone who is friendly and where there is no one to laugh at, or take advantage of, them. It is as if the stories are already begun in their heads, and once started, go on telling themselves. And again and again the first story that children will tell "off the top of their heads" will seem to be their own summaries of life and how they see the world. Sometimes they were also asked, if they could have any story they liked, what story they would like to have— and too often a disadvantaged child's story would begin in a happy blaze of granted wishes, only to quickly accelerate into disaster and loss.

The stories were written down verbatim as the children told them, and were sometimes re-written longhand if the children wanted a copy. The counting necessary for *Far far far far far far far away* (Story 61, p. 98) was recorded by the five-stroke fence-post method. Tape-recording was tried, but apart from the difficulty and error-margin in translating tapes afterwards, it was found that electronic recorders tended to produce more self-conscious "performing" with a view to playbacks, and more concern for speaking than for the content of what was said. Or a shy child just sat while the tape whirred. On the other hand, children seem stimulated by having a friendly adult interested enough in them to write down as they talk. (Adolescents, however, may prefer to tape their own stories rather than face an adult with them.)

Because the stories were recorded verbatim, they may be a contribution to the controversy over the degree to which "disadvantaged" children are handicapped in ability to communicate through limited vocabulary and syntax, poor grammar and few adjectives or abstractions.

Detail of pronunciation has not been reproduced except where the child appears to have consciously or unconsciously exaggerated an effect, as in *The boat going shailing* (Story 53, p. 88). Some stories have been "translated" into intelligible words when children have had severe speech defects, e.g. the story of *Padonga* (Story 1, p. 28) and *Crash* (Story 49, p. 85).

The child's "natural ending" to the story is indicated by the sign /, in instances where he or she has then been asked to continue, with "And what happened?" A curious feature of many disadvantaged children's stories is that they stop in what seems to be mid-air or in the middle of catastrophe. The usual child's "tidiness" and curiosity about "What happens then?" seems absent—possibly because the end, when it is elicited, is so often unhappy, or perhaps because the narrators lack the happier child's enterprise and confidence in finding solutions to the crises they describe.

Most of the stories have been named by the editor. Those story titles provided by the children themselves are given in quotation marks.

Introduction

Heaven lies about us in our infancy!
Shades of the prison house begin to close
  Upon the growing Boy
But he beholds the light and whence it flows,
  He sees it in his joy;
The Youth who daily farther from the east
  Must travel, still is Nature's priest,
  And by the vision splendid
  Is on his way attended . . .

William Wordsworth
Ode on Intimations of Immortality

Perhaps we shield our children too much from reality.

Australian film critic, 1975

This is a book by children, but not for children. Its purpose is to show what happens today to children who are *not* shielded from harsh realities.

It is not realised what these children experience, because there has been no way for them to tell adults except through their disordered and turbulent behaviour—for which a cure is sought rather than understanding and prevention.

In these stories, the children can be heard speaking for themselves.

While more police, guns, counter-violence and limitations of individual freedom are so often called for to counter the "increasing violence of the civilised world", this book looks at the origins of this increasing violence, in the minds of today's children.

These stories have been told to the writer by children with problems—"problem children". Most of them have come from the industrial inner suburbs of Melbourne, Australia, and many are immigrants or the children of immigrants. Living in areas with relatively high rates of poverty, depression and distress, amid general affluence, these children are conspicuously violent, isolated, anti-social or failing. They are at risk of becoming tomorrow's outlaws and misfits, and their stories and drawings show something of how they feel about themselves—and something of the psychological reasons why social problems persist across generations. So many of them seem already destined to be the villains and victims of the next generation—the bashers, vandals, criminals, psychiatric patients, alcoholics, the unemployed and the unemployable, that we must listen to them now, if we are at all concerned that violence and suffering continue amid Western affluence. We should not dismiss what they have to say as trivial because they can only say a little and they cannot say it well—unlike the children whose creative writing appears in anthologies. Any scientist or artist knows how often truth is found through the careful study of small things.

This, we say, is a violent society, which we confidently expect (why the confidence?) to become still more violent. How are children developing to become the violators of tomorrow? Here are stories by boys who are conspicuously aggressive, bullying and destructive even in schools where bashing and vandalism are taken for granted as part of everyday life. Their imaginations are obsessively and even tediously concerned with violence, cruelty and disaster, no matter what the original stimulus to fantasy may be. And it is significant that disaster plays so great a part. These children are not happy bullies who become triumphant kings of the school. The joy of battle for an "average" sort of boy can be felt in stories such as *The dinosaur looking for a fight* (Story 43, p. 78), but the bullies see themselves as mad (Stories 79 and 81, pp. 123 and 124) or evil devils (Story 83, p. 127) who in a very real sense are attacking themselves (Story 84, p. 128).

Who will be the adults who can use violent fantasy as a substitute for action, and who will be the adults who will put violent fantasy into action?

Some features of violent children's stories are possibly significant, because they contrast with others told by children the same age:
1. The lack of variety of themes available to them. Most children can tell violent and even horrible stories, often with relish, but they also have a wide range of other interests, and are not obsessed by violence and disaster.
2. The absence of reason, logic or justice in the universe. Dreadful things happen without explanation or anticipation that could prevent them. Blind forces operate.
3. The central characters are anonymous, without names, usually, and without personalities. The settings are also anonymous, with little interest in the details of the world in which events take place. Boys' stories are more likely to have machines as the central characters long after other boys tend to be more interested in their human controllers.
4. The lack of interest in "what happens then?" Stories can begin and end anywhere, although the usual end is what in another child's

story would call for a continuation to some sort of conclusion. In this regard, as in their pessimism, there is an intimation of adult stories which also reject "tidy endings". The narrator gets his characters into a mess, but has no concern about them after that.

5. The older the child, the less warmth, humour, friendships or sense of values appear in the stories. And when, almost incongruously, there appears a very "soft" story, by a boy about affection for a girl, for example, as sometimes happens, the teller does not want anyone else to be shown the story. (Most children feel rather pleased when asked for this permission.)

It is possible to trace the development of violence and anti-social hatred through the stories of children of different ages. The stories of the youngest boys and girls may be filled with frightening things. The children are cold and starved of love when they are most vulnerable—in real life, emotionally, and often physically, as well as in their stories. As the children grow older, about eight or nine, they begin to identify with the aggressors who have done this to them; they join in on the side of the monsters themselves (foreshadowed in Story 60, p. 95, *Making like the robot*, by Tibor, aged six). Pretty soon, there is little left of the soft core they have grown their shell to hide (see Story 8, p. 34 by a ten-year-old who can only love pigeons), and then that becomes unreachable, or non-existent too.

Very often, possibly always, what happens in reality has already been foreshadowed in the children's stories, as if they were prophecies. The child is indeed the father of the man. Sometimes I see delightful, excessively docile children who live in very disturbed situations, and find simmering beneath their apparent mildness and innocence the sort of feelings expressed by Marietta (Story 68, p. 111) and Mahmoud (Story 69, p. 112). When these children break out, in adolescence or earlier, they may prove to be more permanently damaged than brothers and sisters who have always been loudly protesting little nuisances.

The life-themes that children are developing often seem to be expressed in the symbols of their private fantasies, as well as acted out in their behaviour. Often it seems that they are already foreshadowing their adult life-styles, and that the minds of children of six may be already set in certain directions—towards succeeding or failing, creating or destroying, loving or hating, hoping or giving up.

These stories show how even small children can use, as naturally as they breathe, their uniquely human capacity to symbolise experience that they cannot communicate directly. The use of symbols in many of these stories is in the direct line of all folk-tale and legend.

Myth and symbol are produced by each culture to meet its particular needs, so it has been said. Inner-urban children have their own characteristic themes, not all taken from television. The most distinctive stories told by "disadvantaged" boys, for example, are about the sinking ship (e.g. Stories 52, p. 87 and 53, p. 88), the running boy (Stories 61–65, pp. 98–106) and the tragic mother bird, whose well-meaning mistakes are catastrophic for her family (Stories 23 and 24, p. 52).

The most disturbing and unhappy stories were told by the most disturbed and unhappy children, and they were almost always told without any expression at all—as if they were flat statements of facts, as bald as Norse sagas and as fatalistic. Monsters appeared as if they were everyday realities for the children, and the violence and tragedy of what comes out is beyond any emotion.

In this they contrast with the stories of more fortunate children, who not only narrate with a lively sense of drama, or satisfaction, or humour in their expression, however macabre or dreadful their tale, but have a wide range of themes, exploring every aspect of life, happy and sad. But the more disturbed and unhappy the children, the more restricted their range of themes to the anxieties which obsess them.

It is because of this that to read all these stories in one sitting would be like an overdose. The horror becomes tedious and even trivial, even though short stories have been deliberately chosen, since the longer ones are often only "more of the same thing". Violent stories form an over-high proportion of the several thousand in my total collection. I have therefore tried to show what variety there is, rather than to provide proportional representation.

The stories have been arranged in sections to illustrate how children's imaginations and lives can become stunted and distorted in different ways and with different results. Nevertheless, in some respects the arrangement is arbitrary, since so many of the stories share common features, in theme, or symbols, or environmental stimulus, or the child's response. The emotionally-undeveloped child of twelve can still show much of what he or she was like at four.

Each child is different, although so many problems and so many symbols are shared. Read each story, one by one, as carefully as you might read a good poem, trying to get some feeling of the world which each child knows, which may be very like your own childhood experience, or very different. These stories convey reality in a way not found in children's audience-conscious "creative writing", which has its own stereotypes too, although it can also often reveal more than the trite manifest content indicates.

The content of these stories—given that the children had freedom to tell anything they liked—can also be fruitfully compared with the world's heritage of stories of other ages and cultures; we can consider what sort of material our own culture is offering to children to use in symbolising and understanding and interpreting their experiences. When we see our own world mirrored in children's minds, we may perhaps be able to realise the limitations of the culture that we accept so easily, and the narrow boundaries that we ourselves consent to live within.

The children's stories show the degree to which they have assimilated, as well as turned to their own use, the symbols of our culture and the forms in which feelings and impulses can be expressed.

When the norm is violent and fatalistic, even children without inner personality disturbance may absorb the convention to appear violent and fatalistic, while those who are disturbed may be even more severely affected. There can be a social imperative to be law-abiding; there can also be a social imperative to rebel, to want whatever is forbidden, to bully the weak, and to slash train seats.

This selection of stories shows that children can have stunted or distorted imaginative lives, but the extent of this may not come out fully to the reader, for the simple reason that we are so used to being exposed to horror and despair in the name of entertainment or social reform as we sit in our armchairs, that we can easily be lulled into accepting that children's stories today must necessarily be as tough and doom-laden as the grim old Viking sagas from another grim age.

The only way to open our eyes to realise that the stories here are not "the way it is" or "perfectly natural" is to find what facets there can be in other children's imaginations (see Children who survive, p. 149), in our own and other cultures, and at other times.

Traditionally, nostalgia for the "joys of childhood" has blinded adults to its sorrows, but while still aware of how intense childhood misery and humiliation can be, greater realists can still recollect "trailing clouds of glory", and the "idealistic hopes and dreams of the young". Many of us can remember that in the patchwork of our own early lives, with their bottomless panics and malicious persecutions, there was also sheer happiness, wonder, and the excitement of learning—which so many of these children can grasp only for a few minutes before needing more, more.

Certainly Adam in Paradise had not more sweet and curious apprehensions of the world than I had when I was a child. Victor Gollancz

Index of Stories

PART II What Happens inside Children

I What Happens to Children

THE NEED FOR LOVE

The "loveless personality" can commit any crime, because no feeling towards anyone holds him or her back. It is possible to say that such criminals and psychopaths are born like that, but the histories of many of them show that they were deprived of love as children, so never learned what it was.

Babies who have never had anyone to love them, or have been passed from hand to hand so that any beginnings of love are constantly betrayed, cannot communicate how they feel except by their "abnormal behaviour". The stories here are by older children. Eddie, aged seven (Story 3, p. 29), was such a baby, with a tragic, battered life for his first three years. After that, all the love that adopting parents could give him for four years seemed inadequate, and although long sessions in therapy in an institution for disturbed children reduced his murderous violence so that he could be trusted near other children, he was still a strange boy, as if all his emotions had been flattened.

Other children here still live with one or both parents, but show the sorts of distortions that can occur when parents cannot give love, or are depriving and rejecting, or unpredictably inconsistent, or seem to betray the child by deserting. These stories show the sorts of substitutes for warmth and love some children begin to seek, and the depression and sorrow of others.

The ugly duckling (Story 9, p. 35) was told by a boy who never knew his parents. But there were loving people in the institution which cared for him, and a foster "aunt" who took him for holidays during his first ten years. Although the next three years away from the orphanage saw a series of disturbances in placements, and very disturbed behaviour, the story shows that Mark could still be sustained by the faith that he did belong, somewhere.

Sometimes children are not wanted. Some parents say this openly, while others try to deny it. Often their attitudes are ambivalent or inconsistent. Many parents who thoughtlessly threaten their children with murder or abandonment "don't really mean it", and would be disturbed to find that often their children are not so sure about that. "I'll kill you", and "I'll put you in a home" haunt many children's imaginations, and the wicked witch and the bad giant seem to have some basis in reality. Parents who "believe in being honest" and openly tell the children that they wished they had aborted them, and long for the day that they will leave home, are not sparing the children any hurt either.

Many children react to rejection by becoming violent, disruptive, predatory and anti-social. Others may react to the same situations by becoming withdrawn and isolated. Sometimes they hardly speak. Everything frightens them. They are too inhibited to draw anything except the barest of conventional drawings, or to tell any stories longer than a few phrases. "Boy ... running" or "Girl ... wants her mother". And children can respond to both open rejection and cold pretended love with the feelings of starvation, cold and abandonment expressed in stories such as Linda's.

1. Padonga the Horse

by Linda, seven, a very quiet, pale girl who rarely spoke, and then so unintelligibly that she was receiving speech therapy—to little effect, as she clammed up there too.

She took a while to settle down before she finally drew a horse, a long thin animal with a tail fatter than its body, but once she began talking, the words came quickly although almost incomprehensibly. This transcription is a translation of her very difficult speech, which was taken down verbatim and then decoded later.

It's a horse.
The horse is in a paddock, looking at a wolf,
and it was going to take it to be ate.

He had a broken leg.
And mother came out to see her baby horse and when she see what done,
she runned away.

So mother went out to look for it
and found it dead.

But it wasn't him.
She saw him running away after the wolf,
so mother called it and then it came and went home.
And then it went and died.

(?) It run away after the wolf because it wanted something to eat.
He runned away to its home.
It died, because it didn't have anything to eat.
Both died because didn't have anything to eat.

And it was cold.

2. The Dwarf's Cottage

by Warwick, nine, a runty, mildly retarded freckle-face, whose mother continually complains about him in a loud voice. She declares she has no time or feeling left for him. Warwick likes to set things on fire—particularly the family's own house. His stories can perhaps explain how his desire for a warm home has fused with a flaming anger and desire for revenge. They were all on the themes of being lost and cold, wanting to be found and at home—particularly with Daddy (who is hardly ever home in fact). The boys in Warwick's stories all hated their Mummies, and would never do anything for them.

Warwick has never seen snow, but he has an imaginative understanding of what it means.

That was a little cottage and it was all snowing and
the snow went over the house
and three dwarfs lived there and the mother,
and then a little girl came and saw the cottage,
all snowy and foggy
she got all snow on her
she was cold
and she went inside by the fire, by the heater.

3. Death of the Family

by Eddie, seven, whose adoptive parents said, "We know he doesn't really mean any harm, but we are really afraid that he could strangle his little brother and sister, and at school he hurls rocks, not stones."

Eddie drew a series of stick figures to represent his family, and crossed out each one as the story went on.

My brother die.
My sister die.

My other brother not die. Me die, my father die,
*   my mother die, my other brother die now,*
Me die too, him sick, her sick, him sick, him sick,
*   me sick, her sick.*

4. My Present

by Lisetta, seven, a migrant child who comes to school with welts over her body and legs, "bashed up" by her mother and stepfather for the slightest reason. Her little sister is brain-damaged, possibly for the same reason. At school the only relationship she can achieve with other children is pilfering from them and offering "presents". Most of her stealing seems compulsive and purposeless, until you glimpse what she really longs to be given, to keep and to devour—freely given nurturing love.

A present.
A friend gave me a present . . .
Before I got a Easter egg.
I put it in my bedroom, and when it was Easter I ate it then.

5. Love and Hate—Mother's Day and The Real Bad Witch

by Rosaria, ten, a migrant child who is deprived of most of the things her schoolmates have—spending-money, pretty clothes, lollies, even lunches or lunch-money and, it is often suspected, breakfast. Her cold mother's attitude to her is quite realistically suggested in the stories. Rosaria is often kept home from school to do the work, and then punished for her school failure. Her father is mentally ill, and periodically in hospital.

Her first drawing was of a box with striped paper and a rosette, labelled *This boxs is are Big bresen*. Rosaria's second story was a version of Hansel and Gretel. This is still a favourite with many children, with a particular fascination for fat children, but others also relish the bad end of the old woman who seems to be feeding them the sweet things that they need, but secretly is out to devour and enslave them herself—the bad side of mothers that cannot be openly recognised. In this story Rosaria's anger comes out and she gets her revenge on the mother she could not make love her.

Mother's Day

This box is a present for a Mother's Day,
and it has in perfume and that for the tables you know,
got a vase, and it's got flowers and it got real big thing, real furry coat,
And my Mother will be pleased—she might give me—
she might like me or something,
or be really happy with me.
She might kiss me and she always be kind to me and all these kind of things.

The Real Bad Witch

She's witch and she's real bad and she was real bad,
and this other girl come to her place,
and they was eating sweets and lollipops and all those kind of things,
and she came and said, "Eat more, eat some more things",
but then she changed like a witch and locked them up.
and the girl had to do work for her, and real cruel woman,
and got angry because locked brother up because brother didn't eat,
and then she started laughing and all that stuff,
but when the lady goes, "Go in that fire and get some things",
she goes, "I don't know", so she goes, "I show ya",
So her brother says, "Push her in", so she does and she dies,
so got all the jewelleries and took it to her home and they was very rich.

6. "Lady Like a Flower"

by Debra, eight, whose mother found her very "difficult and hard to love" compared to her younger sister. Debra loved her father, who gave her presents, and she blamed her mother for his desertion of the family. The story gives some idea of how she felt when she was unable to force her mother to love her, yet had nobody else she could turn to. This can explain why, to her mother's further irritation, Debra then misbehaved, instead of trying to win love by being "good".

The drawing was of a "lady like a flower" with large petals all around her head.

Once upon a time there is a lady.
She had a funny face,
she had like a flower
she had many things in her hands
she had flowers.
She was always wanting to have a flower
but one time she thought she never be a flower
but once she growen into a flower
and look how big she is
she's bigger than me
she's bigger than the whole world!
Can't you see?
that I can see

But if I want to climb up her
but every time I climb up her
*   she spits at me and I cannot climb*
and climb at her to go up and speak to her,
*   that's it.*
One time I spit and I shuggled and I punched and tried,
But once I had a idea to punch her
and I got a axe and chopped her
*   and now she is dead.*
And now I can do something about her
I can stick her on the ground
and she can lay on the ground
and I can climb up
She was dead and I climbed up her and that's it.

7. Shootin' Smashin' an' Stealin' and Friendly Mickey Mouse

by Giorgio, eight, a large, clumsy school bully, who is as angry and hostile in school as his migrant parents, after a run of misfortunes, are angry and hostile about everyone and everything in Australia, including their no-good son. Giorgio is very inconsistently treated—alternately belted and pampered by his father, and bribed, slapped and wept over by his mother.

Giorgio told many stories, full of anger, impulsive violence, confusion, alienation and despair—about people rocketing into space and being killed on a strange planet (a common theme with unhappy migrant boys), and about a boy whose response to a teacher's criticism of his work was that:

> *he tore the paper out and he hit lots of kids and he got his knife out and killed the teacher.*

Another boy wanted to learn, but found he didn't like it,

> *so he smashed everything up and felt good, and stoled—he is a stealer.*

When he gets what he wants, his emotions and reactions become even more confused and contradictory—he does not know what to do with success:

> *He wants to take it and give it to lots of people*
> *and they give him lots of money*
> *and he won't give it to them and he busted it*
> *and got out of there and he hit people*
> *and he like hitting lots of people*
> *and he was sad, people were hitting him.*

A child's first and last statements are often the most significant. Giorgio's first story was about a robot, not a real person, who tries to satisfy his needs by violence and stealing. When he makes friends with people he eats them—a devouring love. In his last story, "the story you would really like to have", after all his anger and hostility had been poured out, Giorgio imagines a rebirth, a second start, not as a violent robot, but as harmless, friendly Mickey Mouse, whom everybody likes and who hurts no one. (But still, perhaps significantly, only a humanoid, not a real human being.)

Shootin' Smashin' an' Stealin'

A robot, and he shoot (out of his arms)
and his hat shoots,
and there he shooten a war,
smashed it, he killed the people,
and he smashed all the hospitals,
and he stoled the gold,
and lots of thing.
He had sacks.
He was running away,
and made friends with the people.
He ate them, and that was the end of the story.

Friendly Mickey Mouse

A cartoon about Mickey Mouse.
And he died and he was in fl- in the hospital.
And he is all right.
And he is better and he liked lots of people.
And he was nice and friendly.
That's all.

8. The Crow and the Pigeons

by Mario, ten, whose family relationships are very like Giorgio's, but complicated by bitter culture-conflict, with his Australian mother resisting a Mediterranean patriarchy. Mario is still completely illiterate, dangerously violent, and the bully of a whole school. He is older than Giorgio, and his shell is harder—showing only to pigeons the affection he can give to no human being. Asked to draw a person, he drew a strange mask that filled the page, curiously disturbing with its hundreds of small, obsessive, feathery strokes. Asked to draw anything he liked, he drew pigeons.

Miss, pigeons.
These pigeons flying on over my house, stray pigeons,
and I have a wire net and a trap-door, and pull the pieces of wood out,
and the trap-door don't squash them, just falls on them and catches them.
There's tripler and trebles, the best ones I ever found,
one's a feather-foot, and a friller, and a triple, and a dove,
and a racer, a king and a queen—I've already got those two,
and a big bull pigeon.
and I've got a good cage and a lot of eggs,
and some of the eggs turn out to be sandy pigeons, they're yellow,
and I enter them in the show and they win.

And there's these crows miss, they eat the pigeons if they can get in.
But there was a baby crow, we found it,
and we kept it with the pigeons,
and it grew up with seven young pigeons.

Then some boys, miss, they got in and they killed the crow, miss.
But when they tried to get the crow, miss, all the pigeons
went for them,
and they couldn't get the body,
all the pigeons wouldn't let them.
And the pigeons made movements over it with their wings,
as though they were trying to bury the body.

Mario's other stories were full of blood and monsters, but this is what he said about a picture of a boy:

Can't see what it is . . . can't see what it is . . .
He's in a dark room . . .
looking for a way out.
He's looking round,
trying to think.

Please someone find him and bring him out.
He go home, he glad to get out.

9. The Ugly Duckling

by Mark, thirteen, who spent his life in orphanages and temporary foster-homes.

Once upon a time there was a mother goose who hatched out say sixteen eggs. They all hatched out except one which later cracked, and out popped an ugly duckling. They all waddled to the pond for the mother to teach them how to swim, all but the ugly duckling. He jumped in first and honked.

When the mother and the ducklings went in the water they all had a swim and later on they all climbed on the mother's back including the ugly duckling. The mother knocked him off, and he climbed on again. He jumped back on, only to land in the water again, and he was left in the pond all by himself. Amen/

(How did the story end?)

When he grew up he turned out to be a beautiful swan.

(Postscript. He did. More than once, a child's story has told his future as well as his past.)

SMALL CHILDREN'S FEARS

Even happy children in the most loving families can wake up with nightmares, and have irrational fears about everyday things.

One fear, which we may never really outgrow, but which we learn to deal with in various ways, is the fear of our own lack of control. Children have to learn to control their bodies, in order to learn to walk and talk and play; they also have to learn some control over their feelings and impulses, or they find themselves in danger from the environment and in trouble from the people they disturb.

Some children seem temperamentally to have more trouble than others in learning acceptable ways to cope with anger or frustration. It is easier to destroy than to make things, and it needs self-control to learn to make the harder choice. But a child who at the age of four or even six expresses all his feelings, negative as well as positive, with the spontaneity and lack of inhibition of the child of two or three, is now so much bigger and stronger that his tantrums are no longer as amusing as they may have been to teasing adults who provoked rather than taught him by their example.

Two stories by little boys who throw regular tantrums show how strong is their awareness of the retaliatory consequences, and Lex (Story 10, p. 39) shows how they can even turn their anger against themselves, while Kennie (Story 11, p. 40) is aware that his actions lose him the love that he desperately needs to help him feel more secure.

Three stories describe the panic of small children's nightmares—in these cases responses to environmental dangers. Con's parents do not think he knows that they are planning separation but don't know what to do about Con, since neither really wants him (Story 12, p. 40); Roberto (Story 14, p. 41) is an over-protected migrant boy thrust at four and a half into the horrors of Australian primary school, and Marko (Story 13, p. 40) is a friendless little delinquent wildcat, already always on the run.

10. The Monster Who Takes People's Legs

by Lex, four, who has tantrums.

He's got all legs,
chopped legs off some people and put all on him,
look at the little one,
long leg one.

Destroys everybody.
I can kill him. I'll lift him up then throw him down,
stab him and stab him until all bleeding,
take the legs off the monster.

Lot of aeroplanes in all this big black pointy cloud.
Hiding. Can't get it, cos so deep.
Can't see with their flatelies,
I don't know how they'll get out.

And there's a brown ball rolling down the snow with
  a big brown thing on him.
Can't get out of there.

11. Boy Breaking Down the House

by Kennie, six, referred for "uncontrollable behaviour". The boy in the drawing and story is explicitly himself. He can't control himself any more than anyone else can.

Go thool.
He pu wood and make a door of a house,
make a house.
He'll break the house down,
he'll have no house to live,
he will stay outside,
he stay outside with the cold.
The rain come down,
the snow coming down/
He got to build two houses
five houses
ten houses
twenty
and he will live in the next when one breaks down.

12. A Little Boy's Nightmare

by Con, five, who "cannot concentrate for a minute" at school. The story was about a picture of a boy looking at a trophy.

A cup.
He wants one.
There'll be . . . a ghost.
He runs away from the ghost, and . . .
there'll be another ghost at the other end.
A ghost at both ends.
He'll run anyway.
If he turns the corner
there'll be another one
he'll be trapped
he'll have to stay in the dark,
then when he takes his clothes off and he's asleep

they might take him.

13. Run, Gonna Run

by Marko, nine, a delinquent Greek boy failing at school, whose three wishes would be for—1. A walkie-talkie, 2. A little racing car, and 3. "Be the strongest boy the world, people will pick on you, I'd hit em."

Run, gonna run.
Somebody gonna chase after him,
gonna catch him,
gonna hurt him.

He runs home, he tells his mother.
His mother comes out, the boy's mother told
    the other boy's mother to stop kicking him.

14. New Boy

by Roberto, four and a half, who is still more like a baby than a schoolboy, and cries at school all the time.

That's a robot. Over he goes.
He's come here, he gonna get him, the little boy.
There he is, he gonna get him, cos he's gonna get the little ones,
get his head, got his head, gonna get him in a minute,
and he's at a door here.
Somebody's in here
It's a ghost, it's a ghost, got his arms and little arms,
he's in there—there—umumum,
the big man got him, here across there,
Oh, Oh, you know, that thing came on him and he jump on him,
this way gonna jump on him,
Oh, the thing jump on him. I'm Roberto that's Roberto there.
That's Boog-eyes, where's his eyes, there's his eyes and there his eye.
Oh, Oh, something jump on him.
I do nothing and I jump on him, jump on me
Somebody jump on me
There was jumping on me.

THE OUTSIDE WORLD

In the industrial working class areas of big cities, even when families have everything commercially advertised as necessary ingredients of "the good life"—freezers, colour television, stereos, two cars—the children must still learn to live in an environment with·the highest prevalence of chronic ill health and mental disorder, the risk and reality of unemployment, housing difficulties, anti-social subcultures and gangs and alienated individuals, family breakdown, child neglect, and educational disadvantages increased by the disruptiveness of too many wild children. Even children who are basically not rejected are often and inconsistently maltreated. It is assumed that mothers scream at their children and fathers yell, and that children do not mind the noise.

Inner-city children are more at risk to disorders because the sum total of stresses —physical, social, psychological, economic—to which they are exposed is likely to be greater. In middle-class schools, children are chiefly referred to psychologists because they have specific problems, but the more "socially disadvantaged" the school, the higher the proportion of children with compound vulnerability and multiple problems.

In one typical primary school represented here, the children were 85 per cent immigrant, a third of the Australians did not live with both parents, and 10 per cent received clothing and other needs from the school. During the year, a third of the children left or arrived (excluding the commencing and final grades), and most of the changes were with other inner-urban schools less than four miles away. A third of the new arrivals left again within the year, and children on this un-merry-go-round often trailed referrals to school psychologists, who occasionally caught up with them and their usually insoluble social problems. Over a long period, only one teacher had been known to stay in this school as long as four years.

The five-year-olds often arrived at school with the language and behaviour of under-threes. Most of their early lives had been spent watching television, and working parents had little time or energy to attend to more than outright physical needs. They bought them sweets and expensive breakable toys as bribes and as substitutes for care. As the children grew up in the high-rise government flats, parents faced the dilemma of locking them up, safe but restless and bored, or of letting them loose on the ground and stairs, at risk to bullies, perverts, "bad company" and "getting into trouble".

It is only by Western standards, however, that any of these children could be called economically poor, except relative to other Australians. Few actually go cold and hungry—although some of the children in this book do in fact. But the worst areas in Australian cities cannot compare with parts of Chicago, New York, and other big cities. It is the psychological conditions that damage the children, regardless of social class and subculture.

The next six stories show how children with problems may see the environment in which they live, how anxieties and fears can be increased by the problems of living in high-rise flats, and the dangers of a community in which adults cannot be trusted.

The High-Rise Flats

15. Too Many Things Happen

by Cindy, nine, whose family is unemployed. Cindy already carries a chip on her shoulder, and even good things turn sour for her. Her parents do not know how to fix any of the things that happen to them, and Cindy never expects to be able to do anything either. She expects to be pushed around, and resents it. Cindy's drawing of the high-rise flats looked like a block of battery-cages for hens. (It is not surprising that most small "flats-children" still draw "houses" with fairy turrets and smoking chimneys and little paths and flowers.)

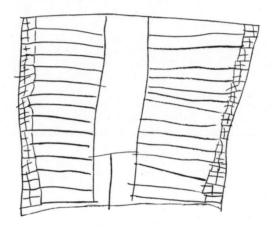

I drew the flats. Some people fall from the flats . . .
Too many things happen
sometimes your taps are not running
sometimes your lift door stuck
sometimes your T. V. doesn't work.
like ours don't work . . .
I don't know much . . .

It's windy and very cold. That's all.

16. Hawks around the Flats

by Adrian, seven, who watches the birds from the nineteenth floor of twenty-storey flats. He can draw and describe the crows, magpies and "all sorts of birds" who come to sit on his window-sill, high up in the air. The hawks are brown and yellow, with curly beaks and white eyes.

Adrian drew the flats like a squared box on pylons, with little people helpless at the windows while the big birds hovered around.

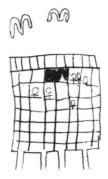

The hawks are flying round the block of flats,
and the people are looking out of the window at the hawks.
The hawks gonna come and attack the people. That's all/

The hawks will kill the people.
There'll be no people left.
The hawks will live by themselves.

17. Suicide from the High-Rise Flats

by Fioletta, eight, who came from a struggling family with an unemployed Italian father and stridently-complaining shift-working mother. The explanation for the suicide in the story is significant—"cos people were shouting always". Children are usually fearful of loud adult quarrels, and in the flats they resonate up and down the windy corridors. Fioletta told a second story about a horse, shot in the leg while its owner was in the "beer bar". The man "called to the house of the animal doctor, but the animal doctor weren't there, so he had to leave it, so it dies". She anticipates no aid for man or beast.

The elevator goes out to there,
When you go out, there's stairs, the door to go up.
Little baby's getting committing suicide.
Santa.
There's the lady coming out. It's all closed.
There's this man he fell out of bed and he went upstairs to the top,
then commit himself suicide,
then going to hit himself there and he's going to bounce off and then he dies.
Cos people was shouting always.
And the police was after him, and he said, "I'll jump if you come over."
Here's the police car/
So they came over, and he jumped.

Rape and Murder

A disturbing number of girls in the inner suburbs, and occasionally boys too, tell stories in which girls are victims of abduction and murder, although girls rarely tell stories about other forms of violence—war, crashes or armed robbery. (Stories 88 and 93 are unusual in this regard.) These victim stories may be the obverse to the boys' aggressive identities. There is also the fact of realistic fears and parental warnings that have a reality basis, since in the "wilder" urban areas and in the high-rise flats children and girls may have little protection from sexual molestation and attack.

The three little girls who told these stories as the first that came to their minds when asked to draw and tell a story were all children whose insecurity was emotional as well as linked to the dangers in their real environment. They were all unloved, aggressive little girls, but Rosamaria was the one who had most of the cards stacked against her.

Although the heroine of *The Pickup* surely had a right to "stand there", there are men who would think she was "asking for it". This may also be true for the little girl who went in the forest "too often for her own good" (Story 86, p. 131) but it also shows a common feature of many of these stories, including Story 20 (p. 47) that even if the girl is saved this time, and even next time too, she will still eventually be caught and die.

18. The Pickup

by Rosamaria, eight, a sniffly, runty, spiderlike creature, the youngest and least wanted child of an alcoholic mother and a father who was never mentioned, if he did exist. When she wasn't being persecuted at school, she was immediately so provocative that even the mildest children were driven to retaliation. She did not seem to have had a chance to learn to be friendly or to trust anyone.

She's standing there.
A man gonna pick her up.
She—uh—her—the man going kill her/
Then the amblelan will come.
Then she'll die.

19. The Man with Lollies

by Penny, eleven, described by her mother as being "an angel-child" until her father became alcoholic and an intermittent visitor in the home. Now her mother cannot stand the sight of her because she is so much the "spitting image" of her father and she has become "that bold you would not believe". Penny had been very fond of her father, but now she was as "vicious" to him as to her mother.

The little girl walking down the street,
and the man hopped out of the car and stopped her
and asked her did she want some lollies.

And the man was going to take her away
and he's going to kill her—and that—
and then he's going to go out
and look for another person to kill/

The man he found another person,
and then he kept on going,
looking for more little children and that to kill.

20. Story of a Girl

by Robyn, seven, a child who, according to her mother, had been a feeble, measly thing with no gumption at any time. Always cold she was and crying at the least thing, her mother had no time for her. She had not been wanted in the first place.

A girl is having a race with a horse—a dog,
and a man came and saw the girl
and wanted to take her away.

And the dog came and bit the man
and then he runned away to his hideout without having any supper,
and the girl patted the dog.

And the man came again,
and the dog bit him again.
and then the dog didn't see him coming
and he got the girl and take her away
and everyone was looking for her but didn't see her.
Then they saw her dead because the man killed her because he was a bad
     man.
Then they found the man and put him in jail.
And that all.

This is Life

Boys often tell stories about organised games, like football, but girls, regardless of social class, often tell stories about playing on swings and slides. The next story could have been told by any little girl aged between six and twelve in any part of Melbourne, and Netta could in fact represent the "average happy girl" from the "average happy home", with very little ever on her mind.

21. Playing for Fun

by Netta, eleven, is a typical girls' "swings-and-slides" story, included for contrast with Marlena's version of the same theme, which follows.

A girl swinging on the slide.
I think she'll be happy sliding down the slide.
Then she went home and asked her mother if she could go to a friend's
    place,
and her mother said, "Yes," so she went to her friend's place,
and played there for a while,
and then went back home,
and she said to the girl,
"Meet you next time, I'll have my dinner now."

22. Playing for Real

by Marlena, eleven, a girl from a very poor, unsettled Australian-Italian mixed-culture family. Her story begins like any other of its kind. But then read on.

There's a swing, and there's nobody on it,
and a slide and people going down,
and a couple of people playing football,
and someone sliding down the pole and pushing the person off the swing,
and one of the things going round and a person pushes you,
and that's a seat with two people and a pram.

And that person there's going to push the person off the swing so she can
    get it,
and the person supposed to be pushing her was pushing her gonna pull
    her off,
that boy just wanted to play football with him so he could take the footbal
and that person there pulled that person off and he's gonna jump on.

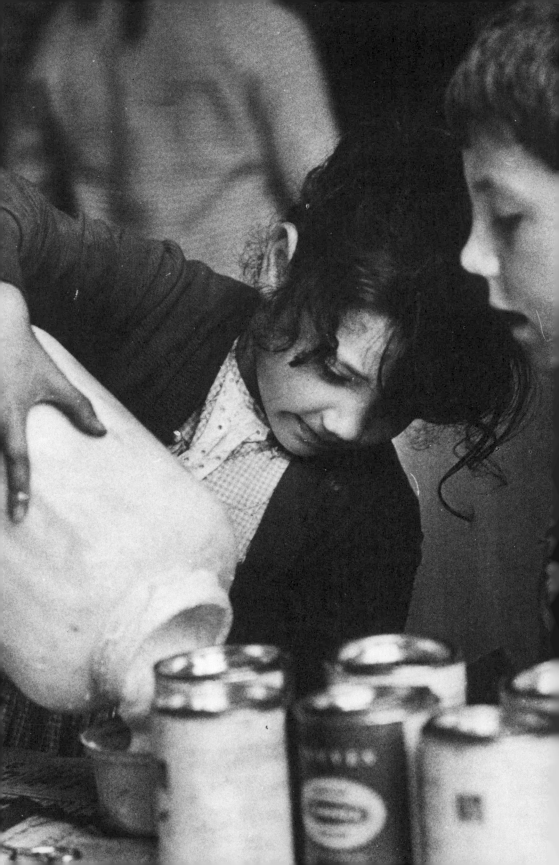

FAMILIES

Helpless and Incompetent Parents

Many children's stories about mothers are very matter-of-fact. Mother is the taken-for-granted person who feeds and smacks. There are also "Oedipus" type stories by boys who seek to replace their fathers, either "marrying" their mothers instead of the rival, who may become a ghost or other shadowy menace, or, more practically, taking the role of mother's boy when father has really gone.

Mummy is very rarely put on a pedestal by these primary-school-age children. There is no danger of that, even when there is clearly a deep mutual love or when the child is desperately seeking love, as in Story 5, p. 30, where Rosaria, a neglected ten-year-old, hopes that her Mother's Day present may persuade her mother to "like me or something, or be really happy with me . . . She might kiss me and she always be kind to me and all these kind of things", while the little girl's own love-hate ambivalence comes out in the story immediately following about the Real Bad Witch.

Children show acute awareness of mothers' inconsistencies and of promises that are not kept. They reproduce the well-worn maternal clichés vividly—a mother "who already talked four times", for example, while they are also quite candid about their own "harping", "whingeing" and "playing up" to get their own way, often successfully.

It is commonly thought that young children believe that their own parents are always right, and know everything. These children have no such illusions. One nine-year-old told about a lady who went to hospital to get a baby, but first she had no milk for it, then she tried to feed it with a cup instead of a bottle and all the milk spilt out and the blankets got dirty. She blamed the baby, but then began to think she might get into trouble herself, so she washed the blankets, and then she did not want the baby to get cold, so she put the blankets on the baby soaking wet, "and when she went to the hospital she got into trouble from the nurses and doctors". Mothers "keep on saying and keep on saying" but the children know that in the end they may just as easily reverse their intentions.

Mothers are weak. In crisis situations they cry, "Oh, what can I do? What can I do?" and in their stories the children try to comfort them, even though they do not know what to do. As in a story by Suzanne, six, who became panicky and uncontrollable when in addition to the "nerves" of her mother at home, the young teacher whom she loved began to show signs of a breakdown too, and eventually left teaching.

And Mummy said, "Oh, what can I do?
Oh, what can I do?"
And the girl didn't know what to do.
'. . . And she said, "Be careful!"
and "If you cry, Father Christmas won't come."
And she didn't know what to do, so she didn't cry.
And she said to her mother, "Susan don't cry."
But Susan cried.

And so children try to comfort their mothers. Quite young migrant children can show compassion for the homesickness and anxiety of mothers who cannot adjust as they can. Many inner-city families have the appearance of the "Australian matriduxy" in which fathers have abandoned all responsibility and the mother is the leader and organiser. But the children may not sense any inner assurance in the women who are running the homes, and there is a distinct genre of little boys' stories about mother birds who for all their heroism make mistakes and cannot save their babies.

23. The Mother Eagle

by Mick, ten, who also told Story 27, *The Drunk Who Caused an Accident* (p. 58).

> *This mother eagle's going down to see if she can find some food for her*
> *   babies,*
> *and gets a rabbit,*
> *and when she's coming back, she drops it down for her babies to feed,*
> *and going down to help the babies feed themselves.*
>
> *And then sees another bird*
> *trying to get the babies, to kill them.*
> *So she takes off to try to stop it*
> *but it gets away*
> *and when she comes back, she finds it's not a bird, it's a plane.*
>
> *And then the bird comes down,*
> *because she thinks it's enemies come down to get the babies,*
> *and the people think it's come down to get the people,*
> *and they got all the people to try to shoot it down/*
>
> *And they did.*

24. The Bird Fallen Down in the Egg and The Mother Bird's Mistake

by Brian, eight, who told "Running Boy stories". Over a period of several months, when I first knew him, he was making a practice of drawing the same thing obsessively all over his school books, even on the covers. These were limited variations on the repetitive theme of thick, stumpy, balloon-headed trees standing up and falling down, with round objects falling out of them. Then on two separate occasions, when he was asked to draw "anything he liked", Brian drew similar pictures, and this and the story following were the stories he told about them, several weeks apart. What lay behind them can only be guessed.

Brian lived in a family that "kept itself to itself", although the boy's mother spent much time waiting outside the school for her two young children. When visited, the home was almost bare of furniture; Brian's mother was friendly enough, but very wary.

The Bird Fallen Down in the Egg

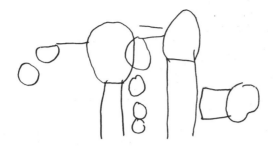

There was a bird,
and the bird fell down in the egg,
the stick broke, and the egg broke,
and the little baby chick was dead from the tree.

Then the bird tried to build another nest,
in a big fat tree so it wouldn't break.
When the baby bird died, the mother bird looked at the chick to see if it was
    well,
and when it wasn't well, didn't know what to do,
so put it back in the nest,
and laid one egg.

So the mother put all wood over it,
so the other birds wouldn't get the germs from the bird.

The next egg, when the tree fell down,
there was a man who chopped the big fat branch.
They chopped the whole tree down,
and three eggs fell down,
and there was the tree fell down,
and all the eggs fell out of the nest.

The Mother Bird's Mistake

It's a bird and a tree.
The eggs are going to fall down.
The mother tried to fly down and took it,
but didn't know one egg was off the tree.
And the tree didn't grow
and the bird came down
and the whole tree fell down.

She thought it was a egg, it was a root, *it helped the tree grow,*
and she took the root.
The bird fall down
the tree fall down
and all the eggs fell down too.

25. Why a Lady Is Sad

by Milo, eight, a boy who seems cheerful enough, though his Maltese mother seems
always tearful or on the verge of tears, and unable with her few words of English to
communicate what is the matter.

Milo told the story about a gay Christmas-card picture of a pretty little maiden
with a cute, smiling baby, sitting in a garden of brightly coloured flowers—a card
someone had given to his teacher for Christmas.

Lady might be sad because hasn't got no food
or no home
or her baby's gonna die
or sick and there's no one around like a doctor,
or she might be sick herself and gonna die,
or had this fever and spread it and gotta go,
or the flowers might be poisonous and he might have to stay there,
or they might bite her and that,
she might die because no food, and stay there
and her baby die too.

Inconsistent Parents and Chaotic Family Life

26. Life with Mother

by Oresteia, eight, who was misbehaving in showy ways, and failing dramatically
at school. Her parents showed no concern, and had never visited the school, even
on occasions when all the other children in the class had had at least one adult coming
on their behalf, including other parents who like hers, were on alternating shift
work and hardly ever saw each other. The children were left with neighbours during
the overlapping times when both parents were absent; Oresteia disliked these neighbours intensely, although her sister seemed unaffected.

In the story Oresteia seems to be trying to come to terms with the differing sets
of confusing values and attitudes of inconsistent adults and the differences between
statement and action, reality and desire. The story is hardly accurate in its details,
but it describes very clearly the atmosphere in which many children grow up, and
the emotional problems they face when parents are inconsistent and impulsive—
like themselves.

Mothers often talk about their most private affairs and about their children in
front of the children themselves, as if their children could not understand, or were
deaf—but stories like these show how sensitive the young child actually is to parents'

feelings and problems. There is the description of the mother hiding, frightened and crying in the bedroom because she fears she has hit her child too hard—and this is not an uncommon situation.

But the children learn too much. When they grow up, they tend themselves to repeat the same child-rearing patterns. Even in the stories they tell as children, this is foreshadowed, when they mix up who is the mother and who is the child. This confusion is possibly even more significant than the shifting identities of the children in the stories—are the stories really about themselves or can they pretend they are about somebody else?

A mother has a beautiful baby and she always takes care of it,
and she rocks him and says a song like Rock My Baby,
and she really loves her baby because he's so beautiful,
and if he do something wrong, his mother sometimes hit him,
but most mothers don't hit their children because they love them so much,
    and love to kiss them.

Sometimes they break things real much,
Mother says don't do that,
and when they grow up they go to school, and say he's very sick
the mother don't know, but God punishes them,
and God punish them do something wrong.

Maybe one day the mother believe do something wrong,
the big kids do something wrong when they don't want to go to school,
the mothers sometimes hit them and say you just lazy, you lying,
Sometimes mothers hit kids on the head and God sometimes punishes the
    ladies, the fathers.

*Sometimes mothers take children, sometimes children say the truth they
    want to stay home,*
*sometimes mothers let them stay and they go out to the park and have nice
    things.*

*Mothers love their children and take them out but only when they say the
    truth*
or the mothers hit them. They always say the truth.
Then mothers they say you better go to school
*so they learn and children love sometimes go to school to learn and
    sometimes learn to do writing,*
*and sometimes if really angry they say bad words to your mother and the
    mother hits them because not good,*
*and when sometimes the children are really angry they hate their mother but
    their mother still loves them,*
*and the mother if something happen to the children or another person hits
    them she'll hit them back*
*because her kid had to go to the hospital and she really loves the kid and so
    she tells the kid who hit her little kid to stop hitting it and her mother
    says I'm going to tell the teacher and you'll get kicked out of school,*
*and after when the baby is good and out of hospital you don't go after
    other boys or girls so they can't hit you,*
*and the little kid does what his mother has told him, done what she wants
    him,*
the mother says you're a good little kid,
*but the child really angry and says I hate you Mum and says bad words
    and the mother hits him and punish you and not watch TV and go to
    school every day, if you're sick you've still got to go.*
The baby cries and the mother feels sorry because she's hurting the baby,
and she says, All right, I'll forgive you this time but not next time.
*Baby says All right, I'll let you this time go but next time if you do
    anything wrong I'll punish you again,*
*so the baby goes all right, I won't do that again, so the mother forgives the
    child,*
and the new little kid was beginning to be nasty
and the mother beginning to hit him all the time,
*and one day the boy was really good and the mother thought he done
    something wrong and punished him and the little kid didn't do nothing*
so the mother said, Didn't you do anything? and the kid said, No, I didn't,
*so she kissed the kid she gave him some money and said you can go
    anywhere you want.*
I'm going to let you have a free day, because you're the best boy in the class,

and she went to the teacher and said, is he the best boy in the class?
And the teacher said No, I mean Yes, and the mother was really proud of
the kid,
because he was really good, and punished him the other day and she felt
really scared and went in the bedroom and really cried because she hurt
him,
and the next time he was a really bad boy and went to the teacher and the
teacher said No,
and she went back to the house and hitted the boy really really hard
and hitted her until the morning time
hit the girl and the boy maybe
and then he went to school,
and after all the time he was really really good
and never done anything wrong again
because if he was, his mother would hit him again,
hit him and hit him and hit him,
and she went to the teacher, Is he really good? and the teacher always said
yes,
and she got fish and chips from the poor boy and stoled them,
the mother said, Give them back you dirty thing
and he didn't,
the boy was selfish, so his mother said, All right, I'm going to hit you really
hard, morning until night time,
morning until night time
morning until night,
hit him 21 times and the boy was sick
he wasn't sick but he was crying every day,
and said I'm not going to do anything.

Saw some people eating fish and chips,
he didn't snatch them off and said to his mother,
Mum, please buy me fish and chips too, and his mother said,
All right, you a good boy, I'll buy you how much you like.

His mother said, you're a very good boy, and the boy was very good and
never, never told lies or bad words or hitted his mother or other kids at
school,
maybe a good little kid was stronger,
and his mother wouldn't even hit him.

And the mother bought another baby, and the boy said, I'm not going to hit
him any more because he's the most beautiful baby there ever was,
and when he growed up there was two girls and one boy,

The kid said, I like you, and once they went to the fish and chip shop
    and saw another kid eating fish and chips,
and asked his mother and he gave him some of his and the boy was really
    proud and all, and the other kids liked playing with him,
and that's why the mother loved the little kid, because really nice and never
    told lies and the little boy first nasty and then been good,
and loved his mother and sister and father and they were very good and
    did not say lies again because really good to each other.

27. The Drunk Who Caused an Accident

by Mick, ten, a quiet, friendly little boy, normally "no problem at all", but at the
time of telling this story, his teachers could "do nothing with him, suddenly he's in
trouble about everything". He had been away for a few days with no reason given,
and there seemed to have been a recent disturbance in the family that none of them
wanted to talk about, but it was clear he was acutely emotionally upset, felt something
terrible had happened, could not understand it, and felt that somehow he must have
been bad for it to happen.

The story begins with Mick as the central character, who then becomes the drunk
who innocently causes a fatal car crash simply by being there, in the wrong place.
And the car occupants themselves have innocently killed an old lady, without realising
that she had even been hit, and she died, as so many people die in children's stories,
because help did not come in time. And before that, a joke at a party had started
off the fatal chain of events, and after that, when punishments came, it was the
wrong man who was imprisoned for life. It is as if Mick feels himself to be in a situation
in which he is innocent but feels himself to be guilty and seen to be guilty—as children
often feel when unpleasant things happen which they may have in some moment of
spite half-hoped would happen. It is as if their wishes are to blame.

There's me
and there's this policeman.
and he saw this drunk man coming along the road
and this policeman said, "I'm going to go after them,"
and they were going to a party,
and the lady said not to stop because they had to get the coffee,
and this character goes on standing in front
and there's a crash
and there's glass everywhere, and it hit him,
and all the blood fell out.

And one car had a seat belt in front,
and the baby fell out,
and the policeman comes, and then the policeman said,
"If it wasn't for you, it wouldn't of happened."

Because they didn't know
before they nearly hit the man, that they hit an old lady,
so when another car came,
then that lady comes round and looks around,
and the man goes for the ambulance,
and then they found the old lady,
but she died because they didn't get there in time.

But the baby was still alive,
So they said, "Give it air and give it blood,"
but it died.

The man, before that, was at a party,
and for a joke put brandy instead of beer,
half brandy, half wine,
and this *man found out*
and this *man got his life in jail*
and the other man got nothing.
The other man said, "If you tell, I'll kill you,"
so he didn't tell|

He's drunk, and after that wouldn't walk properly,
He kept on falling over.
And this is what happened crossing the road

28. Such is Life

by Danny, ten, who lives with ailing grandparents, and only visits his parents and brothers and sisters sporadically. He is quite intelligent, but has already repeated a grade, and is still far behind. He sits in the classroom looking impassive and miserable and does nothing unless the teacher gives him undivided attention; he stands in the playground looking impassive and miserable. His Nana takes him to and from school, and "lives only for him". Granpa is bedridden and Nana and Danny are often sick in bed too.

My father when he was only a little boy
and he was at his friend's party
and he's blowing one of them things go up and down
and my Nana makes them
and then they have a fight
and my Dad gets a broken nose
and the other man gets a black eye
and my Dad blows the whistle into his face
and then his friend throws the cake into his face
and then they start fighting and my friend came in and broke up the fight
and then my Dad started fighting on him
and broke his jaw
and then the man broke his hand
and then my Dad had to go to a hospital and found that he had a broken
*   arm*
and all his T-shirt was covered in blood
and then he went home
and the dog bit him
and had 21 stitches in his head
and then the dog attacked me
and I had to have six stitches in my head
and then my little sister threw a bottle at him
and cut his head open
and then the dog bit her
and then fell on the floor
so I got a belt
and hit her
because
she killed the dog
and then my Dad came home
and belted her

and the dog was buried in the back yard
and then the other dog ran away
and got ran over
and then my nephew's cat died
and then we had bury two of the dogs,
and then we made a cross for it
and then we put all our names
even our other cat's name
but that didn't die
and then it hopped on the window
and smashed the glass
and when the glass broke the cat went through and fell in the mud
and then we had to go out the front
and got it out of the mud
and wash it and then my little sister put
dirt all over it
so we pulled
her nose
and sent her to bed
and then it ran away
to my auntie's place
and so I went to my auntie's place
and brought it back
for my brother
and then it ran away again
and we couldn't find it
that's all.

Separated Families and Divorce

29. The House with the Beautiful Poplants

by Shaun, nine, whose life has been a series of broken homes, placement in institutions, retrieval for a new start in the family again, give or take one or two of its previous members, and then the whole cycle over again. A few weeks after he told this story, Shaun's father was once again in jail and the little peaky-faced boy was again in an institution, "just in time to be an angel in the Nativity Play", as some kindly person said. At school he was no angel. He was aggressive and thieving and seemed very tough.

His drawing was a conventional child's house surrounded by the usual large conventional flowers. His second story was of a ship, "sailing on a sunny day". It sank.

A house, with flowers all round the house, and with poplants,
and trees all round the house, and people come to visit the house.

And then some people lived in it.
And then they said, "We will never leave."
And then they stayed there, and when they died, their daughter lived there.
And when they went to bed, it was raining, and the poplants got wet,
and in the morning, the poplants were very nice, beautiful flowers.

And then one night somebody went to see the house.
They picked all the flowers.
And the police got on to it and then they went to jail,
and the police said, they're never going to leave the police station.
They had to stay there.

Then they died.

And then the police felt sorry about the beautiful flowers.
And when they got here, well, they went to church and then they put in
*   money, and they put money in—*
and then they died.
and then they had to pull the house down.

Then that was the end.

30. Birdie Hatched out of an Egg and The Bad Son

by Brendan, five, who was being extremely violent to other children at school. He told his first story when his parents were planning separation but "had not told the little ones". His drawing then was of a pathetic baby bird in a nest, and he told a story of how it flew away to live a life of its own.

Birdie Hatched out of an Egg

Little birdie and he hatched out of an egg
he's in the gun trees.
He will fly away.
He'll put leaves in a nest with some babies and they'll hatch.
nobody else. He'll just live,
just live in the nest.

A year later, Brendan's aggressiveness had again reached the limit that teachers
could tolerate. His parents were separated, the divorce case was about to be heard,
and Brendan was blaming his mother for refusing to take his father back again. His
first drawing then was of a tortoise with a great strong shell and secretive smile, and
the story about the tortoise was that nobody could get it to come out of its shell because
it didn't want to. Then Brendan drew a "Princess Mother", a "King Father", and
"Son" who stood between them, joining both their hands. In the story, he seemed
to be describing very mixed-up feelings about his mother, and to be blaming her
for his own violence, as well as feeling guilty for it himself. But if only the family were
all happy together, he thinks that he would never feel bad any more.

The Bad Son

by Brendan, six.

A Princess, she had some gold.
About the King's Wife, and the son who always never changed.
They lived in a tall castle, they were tall giants,
and their son was bad.

He all he tried to stone, threw a stone at a witch,
but she hit her head with a stone, on the witch's head,
and the witch turned him into a baby dragon,
and every day his friends all came to laugh at him,
and threw water in his mouth so they can't get burnt.
And then they lived happy ever after.
Then the witch came back and she was sorry.
She turned him back into a boy and he was sorry,
and he was never bad any more,
and they lived happy ever after,
Mary Queen
Father Jumbo
and Little Boy Queen.

31. The Worried Squirrel

by Robert, ten, whose teachers considered him a quiet, average sort of boy—perhaps a little too quiet. He introduced himself to me with "I'm Robert—my parents were divorced two weeks ago." The drawing and story "of anything you like" show how completely he described himself and his feelings about himself in that concise introduction.

I like drawing trees like my friend does. I like drawing things on fire.
That little squirrel is looking for a shelter, and then he sees the broken-down
*   house*
because he wants to shelter from the fire.

I put in the lightning, and there's an explanation for the fire.
And it's a thunderstorm, and he doesn't like thunderstorms, so he's going to
  get in the broken-down house,
He's wondering how he's going to go, because he can't get down from the
  tree,
He can't get down from the tree because it's all on fire, and his hole's too
  high and he's worried.
That's all/

(How does the story end?)

I dunno. Spose the house will get on fire
and all the tree will go on fire
and the squirrel will die.
Because when I draw my pictures like that, I always draw all the rest of
  the picture on fire.

Typically in children's stories, the children are often wiser and cleverer than the adults—although there are usually one or two adult demigods for security. The difference with these children is the degree to which this perception is true—children plead with their parents not to fight each other, not to drink so much, Daddy not to beat up Mummy, not to commit one desperate act or another. Nobody has to teach these children that this is a world that has been messed up by their elders. There are never any demigods.

32. The Boy Who Cried "Don't Shoot!"

by Greg, nine, whose parents had broken up three months before. Superficially, Greg seems unaffected, although he has been referred for tantrums and school failure.

A plane flying
and it's got its—
it's shooting another plane, and there's a little boy watching the plane
  shooting,
and one of the planes fell down and just missed the boy,
and then he ran home—
real sad
the man in the plane got shot
and when he was shooting, the boy said, "Don't shoot,
Stop, Come down and make friends!"
And they wouldn't listen to him.

33. The Father of the Little Princess

by Carmen, eight. When Carmen's father went back to Malta and never came back, Carmen put the blame on her mother and refused to live with her again, and to her mother's great distress, managed to get pitying cousins to take her in. Meanwhile the story shows how she was trying to romanticise the situation in fantasy.

Little princess.
One day the little princess' father had to go to this war,
and this little princess never knew.

And her father was killed in the war.
And that's it.

34. The Father Who Murdered His Family

by Leanne, fourteen, who wanted desperately to live with the father who had deserted, even though he was quite indifferent to her. Leanne did eventually leave home and began modelling herself on her father's delinquent way of life, so that she was soon in trouble with the police.

People are going for a drive—this is true—
what happened to my girl friend—used to be my girl friend—
had cancer—going to Sydney to pick up the other children, seven of them,
and they're going along the Hume Highway,

and the taxi . . . oh, we'll pretend that's a taxi—
and the driver, which was her father, threw her mother and her out of the
* car,*
opened the door and they fell out,
and they fell down the cliff and they both were killed.
They were rich, and he got the inheritance, all the money,
so all the kids were from fifteen and under,
and they're all in a orphanage and that.

35. Boy Put in a Boys' Home

by Francis, seven, who was talking about what he knew, for he had been in the boys'
home for a week. Francis' story is quite complex and can be read on more than one
level. Why is a boy put in a boys' home? Because he has done something bad. This is
a very common feeling children have when adults abandon them.

The little boy cries for his parents, but then courageously tries to face his situation
and make the best of it, trying to make other human relationships "and he won't
break it" (a clue to what the cup represents to Francis). But then he spoils it by
playing with it in the mud (an early initiation to what some of the boys are already
teaching him), and when a friend lets him have the love and trust the cup symbolises
—"Don't break it", poor little Francis finds it will break in spite of himself.

He's looking at the cup
cos he wanted to keep the cup.
He'll get caught by the police.
He'll go in a boys' home
then he will cry for his Mum and Dad.
Then he will stop crying because there's good boys there and he wants to
* play with them*
and then he will make friends with them.

And then he will say to his friends if he can play with somebody
and then he'll play with them
and he won't break it.
And then he played with it in the mud (laughs)
and he will say to his friend, "Can I keep the cup?"
and his friend said yes, and then he said, "All right",
and then his friend said, "Don't break it, because I made it",
and then one of the handles break and then he sticked it with glue and then
* his Mum was happy,*
and his Mum put it up high in the cupboard
and then he went to get it down
and then he got on a chair and got it and then he took it and played with it,
and then his sister said if he can play with it,
and he said that . . . to his sister that you can play with it but don't break it.

WHEN CHILDREN ARE LABELLED

36. The Boy They Wouldn't Bail Out and The Bank

by Les, eight, who was referred for "inability to tell the truth" and because "he seems to believe his own lies". He was the indulged "afterthought" child of elderly parents whose other children were now all married. He was given plenty of pocket money "so he won't want to get into trouble" and he seemed to have every advantage. Les showed a fertile imagination in making up stories in any situation. Although, curiously enough, most of the tales he made up seemed to be involved with stealing, his behaviour showed his potential to become a charming confidence man rather than a housebreaker. It is quite likely that his parents have at some time in desperation threatened a boys' home for him—it is a common though ineffective and potentially damaging attempt at discipline, which tends to loosen the emotional bonds tying children to their families.

The bank was "the story you would like to have". He started off owning the bank, but apparently that was not exciting enough.

The Boy They Wouldn't Bail Out

This boy he stole some money out of a shop
and put in a boys' home
and his father and mother were taking and putting him there
and he was mad at them.

And he wants to get out, and asking if they could bail him out
*   and really sad,*
and calls friends together, and they get a plank, and all try to get the steel
*   bars down and he got out*
and he went out
and they said, "What are you doing home?"
and he said, "Somebody bailed me out, I don't know who."

And they took him back
and left him there
and they didn't bail him out
because they didn't want him back again.
That's the end.

The Bank

Have a bank. Own a bank.

About a bank that had fifteen billion dollars, and a man robbed it one night.
And he took all the 5200 dollars, and there was about 200 dollars left.
And they couldn't afford to give all the other people their money back,

and so they all went to the authorities, and about two or three years later
    they found him and he had spent all the money.
And the police said, "Get all the money back.
We don't care where you get it from,"
and hold his arrest two months.
And he made another bank robbery and got the money.

And the manager of the first bank was waiting for him and then he
    clobbered him, and he had all the money stuffed in his pockets and that to
    put back into the safe.
And they held him arrest for a life sentence,
and they got all the money back.

37. The No-Good Robber

by Clark, ten, a mildly retarded boy whose realisation of his inadequacies made
him so hopeless that he was wrecking his chances of using the little that he did have.
He was persecuted by the other children in the playground, and could not do the
work in the classroom.

   Adults may not realise that most mentally retarded children, outside institutions,
are very aware of their limitations—they may be dull, but they are not blind. These
children often "under-function" because they can no longer stand the humiliation
of always trying, and always failing. Some of them maintain a protective grin, but
some like Clark shamble more because of their poor opinion of themselves than
because of poor motor co-ordination.

   (The last time I saw Clark, however, he was walking tall. He was now attending
a school in which he had found friends, and where the teachers had discovered that
he had a knack for mending things.)

   Clark's picture, drawn while he was still a butt for all, was of a boy with rabbit-
ears and no hands or feet.

Funny. Silly.
Robbing the bank. Going to clout somebody on the head
they just drop down
he runs away
the police catch him.

His legs are short, skinny.
He's mean, naughty, doing bad things.
He's called John and he's ninety-nine.
He's got no family, he runs away every time.
Nobody likes him.
He's a robber.
He goes to sleep in a dog's kennel.
The dog'll bite him and lick him and tell him to get out of his dog's
   kennel.
He gets into trouble, bad trouble.
Nothing can be done for him.
The police catch him, put him in jail.
He don't like it.
He got no house. He has to live on the ground.
He likes nobody.
He wanted to steal things, to take things, take money to buy things, to buy
   his own house . . .
a flat to put all his things in there what he's got.
He got a truck he robs things with.
He run away because he's no good.
Nobody wants him to stay/
He can't hear. He sees nothing. All he does is drive his truck.
Can't think of any more.

II What Happens inside Children

DREAM AND REALITY

Children are often assumed to be insensitive, tough, or are "too young too understand" because they may give no outward sign of being affected by some of the horrible things in their lives.

However, their fantasies show what is really happening to them, and what perhaps is more significant, how their futures may be affected through the picture of the world and their place in it which they are developing. Children's imaginations move rapidly between the real and the dream, now and the future. In the stories of Rosaria (Story 5, p. 30) a realistic account of her attempt to win her mother's love with a present was followed by the fairy-tale fantasy of revenge on a wicked witch who hated children; Giorgio's robot and Mickey Mouse (Story 7, p. 32) both came from television—could he tell you if either were real?

Fantasies are not necessarily "catharsis"—they may merely parallel reality at different levels. The next two stories show clearly how children (and adults) can live in two worlds at once.

A typical six- or seven-year-old boy may draw a rocket and describe its take-off and round-trip to the moon with as much technical detail as he can muster, and follow it with "John's birthday", when everyone will give him presents and they go to the park and play on the swings and the seesaw and the slide.

Other children are not so fortunate, either in reality or imagination, and tell stories like Raymond's *Father and son* (Story 55, p. 91) or Damian's *Reality and dream* to describe their disastrous experiences of life.

38. Reality and Dream

by Damian, seven, a mildly retarded hyperactive boy failing at school.

Reality	Dream
Name's John.	*Our car*
He fall—hard	*cars go faster*
hit a wall	*going go crash, crash in the pon*
hit the bricks	*boat comes along*
hit a fence	*car gets crash*
hit bike	*boat goes on the water*
go faster	*boat crash*
it break	*car crash in the boat*
bump head	*car turns around*
	car goes on the road
	crashes
	car
	crashes

LONELINESS

When rejection is absolutely undeniable, and when for whatever reason children are abandoned to institutions, how resilient are they?

39. The Dragon's Last Stand

by Harold, seven. Less than a week in an orphanage. It was his first experience. His stories show how he was "adjusting". His mixed-up reactions showed themselves in unpredictable changes of mood and behaviour, and his first story showed his angry feelings of desperation, like a cornered monster. He must be a monster, to be so unlovable that people would do this to him—but he still nurtured dreams of rescue from oppression, and told the story of Cinderella that is so often told by oppressed children as well as indulged in by the more fortunate, and he told it in its soft "feminine" form with all its romantic fairy-tale trimmings. Harold's first drawing was of a monster with sharp spiked back, scorpion tail, protruding eyes, and red coils of smoking breath; his second, of the fairy-tale princess, looked more like a very motherly person—the sort who could mother little boys rather than allure a prince.

Don't know any stories. I can't tell a story because I don't know what it
* is ...*
He's killing people—they've been trying to kill him.
They're throwing spears—he's spitting out fire.
He's stepping on people.
He's hitting them with his tail.
That's all|
He's going to be dead.
He's dead.
He's dead now.
That's the end. Because he's dead.

How do children feel when there seems to be no one who really loves them and they are really alone in the world, because their experience is that everyone will let them down, sooner or later?

40. The Donkey

by Sharlene, eight. Sharlene was the prettiest girl in the class, and although she was a bit behind in her schoolwork, her books were neat, and at least she could read. She was well-behaved, at least when the teachers were looking.

Sharlene had been at the school for four days. She had been at the school before, a few years ago. In fact, she had been to eight schools, some twice and even three times.

Nobody wanted Sharlene. Neither of her parents wanted her, and she was farmed out to relatives and acquaintances, moving on from one to another as she became inconvenient, or possibly, as the story suggests, she "bucked". She will say in a matter-of-fact way that nobody wants her, so she always keeps everything in a suitcase for when she has to go away again.

Four days later Sharlene went off again. The social worker who follows her movements then appeared, and discovering she had left, finally tracked her down at another school not far off.

Sharlene's drawing was of a donkey, copied from a library book she had been looking at, with pictures of animals.

> *The donkey was standing, for someone was . . .*
> *He had dropped someone else, they had dropped him because they didn't like him*
> *and he was looking for someone else—sadly.*
> *And he didn't find someone, and he walked a bit,*
> *and a little boy came, and he smiled at the little donkey,*
> *and he said, "Did you buck him off or something?"*
> *and he nodded his head like that, as horses do,*
> *and he got on him and rode him around,*
> *and took him back to his owner—*
> *he took him back home and his mother said,*
> *"Take him away,*
> *take everything off him and take him away,"*
> *—because they didn't like the colour of it,*
> *and they burnt it up because they didn't like it,*
> *and that was the end of the story,*
> *the donkey died*
> *got killed by a hunter,*
> *the pony walked away sadly and got killed by a hunter.*

41. Lost in the Streets

by Sergic, nine, a migrant boy with "everything" against him. At his fifth school in his short life, teachers found him "very aggressive and disturbing in class, and learning nothing". He was in that nobody-cares-land of being "not backward enough for Special Schooling and not bright enough for normal school". After one term, his unstable family shifted house again, and this lonely, neglected boy had to face more battles in another strange place. Sergic's first story was a violent one, like

Giorgio's (Story 7, p. 32) and like Giorgio, he followed it with another showing his vulnerability. First he tried to imagine a great strong castle and a great strong giant, people who could be on the attack and not the victims. However, once his story was under way, his picture of what life is really like took over. There are naughty men, there is an enemy castle too, and as fast as one lot of people get killed, the killers are killed too, and the giant himself topples. Then it stops. Temporarily, until the tragic sequence happens all over again.

The pathos of Sergic's second story, given below, reveals more about why he is developing the tough, fatalistic attitudes that he shows in his behaviour as well as in the account of the Giant's Castle. This is the way he experiences the world; lost in a strange place and looking for a friend he does not have, the boy is not recognised by others as being a human being at all. They only see him as a small, helpless creature, and humans have no pity for what is small and helpless. He is as usual misunderstood, and, as usual, killed. Living in a world like this, it is not surprising that Sergic tries to identify with giants and strong castles and take revege, even though giants, however big and bad, also have no chance in the end.

That person is going to his friend's place and
then he had to go to a different place
and he got lost in the town
and then when some people come they thought he was a bird
then they come with a gun and killed that boy
and the policeman came and told him which one did he kill
and he said, "I killed a bird"
and the policeman came around there he found the boy dead/
He collect his mother, a few days he was dead.

42. The Dinosaur Who Was Got At

by Shane, eight, another boy who felt cornered, fighting for his life against the hostility of the world. He was the youngest of four brothers, one of whom was removed from the custody of his parents by Court order because he was a battered baby. At home he was knocked around by a moody alcoholic father, and his attendance at school was irregular, with absences seeming to coincide with mornings when "Mum was a bit tired and didn't get up."

At school he gave the impression of being a solitary boy, unable to remember anything, "very gentle and slightly fey, but able to defend himself with a good deal of force if he feels attacked. The Shane we see at school tends to be good and unobtrusive—the Shane we hear about from the flats is a well-known 'naughty boy'. One fears for his future. . . ."

Shane was receiving speech therapy because of his severe language difficulty—here was one thing the helpless authorities could try to do for him. He was intelligible when he told this story, because he told it with long pauses, spitting out the single words.

A dinosaur.
The dinosaur got burnt up.
He was dead.
And they chucked spears at him.
Then they ate him up.
The end.

43. The Dinosaur Looking for a Fight

by Menelaus, seven. For contrast, here is a typical dinosaur story by another inner-urban boy. Menelaus is also fascinated by dinosaurs, like most children in this age group, and from the security of a loving home he can sally forth to enjoy the rough-and-tumble which is for him part of the fun of growing up to become a man.

A dinosaur rocking along in here, and this cave-man thing.
And it's kind of going to attack another dinosaur.
This one's gonna win.
Then it'll go back to his place where he come from.
He's walking along to find one to fight.

44. "Fred"

by Lee, ten, a middle-class boy failing in schoolwork although he was quite bright, and failing in everything else too. He professed no interest in anything, and his usual response was a shrug.
"What do you do at playtime?"
"Scuff my feet and make patterns in the dust."
Lee's parents have been separated for some years and have shuffled off most of the responsibility for the boy on to grandparents and aunts.
Although his story is "middle class" in its concern with the personality and feelings of the hero, it is "socially disadvantaged" in its senseless violence and pessimism. He drew an ugly youth with pimples and clawed fingers.

He's probably scratching someone—
or putting his hands out.
Someone died—cos he kind of looks sad in his eyes and that.
He's putting one foot over against his other shoe.
Probably a relation's died or someone.
He's nervous.
someone could have shot him
and could have been going for him next, because in his family or suthing
He thinks he's gonna get shot and then he'll die.
Just doesn't tell you.
He gets shot—

he only gets injured,
but the police find him
and shoot him in the head and kill him.
But he's only injured.
Because he called some life-guards over,
thought it'd be too late, but they got there when he was going to fire his
*   second shot.*
He went real scared to his house.
He got pimples.
He's a person everyone picks on and that.
With a big business.
His father died and give him his will with all the money and that|
He's saved and taken to hospital,
and he's O. K. then.

45. Australias Loses the War

by Gregg, eight. We have all met the kid whom nobody likes, and who tries to impress by grandiose lies about his relatives and adventures. Gregg was a boy who was persecuted by a school gang; nobody ever believed his grand tales. In a private situation, his stories were still fantastic, but they had this truth about them—like Gregg's own battles, they ended disastrously.

Once there in 1974 my uncle went into the army and he was in an
*   aeroplane and he was fighting Japanese.*
He was Australias and he was a pilot.
He had fifteen tons of bombs and he let em all off.
The aeroplane exploded and my uncle came down in a parachute and got shot.
So the Japanese had won the fight, and Australias were all killed.

The end.

ALIENATION

Alienation is a common theme in unhappy children's stories. Today it is often expressed in stories about robots or space. Children of unhappy migrant families are particularly likely to tell stories about explorers who go out in rockets to colonise new worlds and find the planet is poisoned or blows up on them or there is no air or food. Milov's story of the Moon Creature is the same theme in reverse. Here it is the earthmen who have captured the hapless, helpless, horrible creature from the moon, destroyed it and thrown it away, and only its skeleton is exhibited in the museum for the uncaring mob.

46. The Moon Creature

by Milov, nine, whose family had been in Australia for four years, and still could not settle anywhere; Milov himself was delinquent out of school and defiant in it, not learning anything although obviously clever, and unable to mix in with the other boys at all, even the other migrants. It is significant that the "person" he drew was not human.

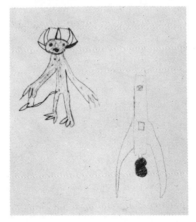

It's a rocket,
and it's just about blasting off to the moon,
cos they're going to the moon
for the reason that there's some kind of creature,
and they're going to catch it
and put it in a space rocket
and made a statue of it
and put it in the museum
so other people can come along and see the creature.

And the real creature they caught,
they'll kill it and throw it away,
and take the skeleton and put it into the museum too.

It's a monster,
and has toes
and has fits—got those sort of wires
and got sharp ears
and sharp eyes
and fingernails and legs
and it's skinny and got dots all over it and got a horrible tail,
and it hasn't got a house to live in,
so they make a sort of little cave,
and that's where they sleep.

47. Lost in Space

by Jackie, ten. This is a typical space story. The title comes from a popular television serial, which does indeed include tragedies in it, but not to the extent that so many stories told by children do. Characteristic features of these stories are a first disaster which is overcome, and a second one which is overwhelming; some error of judgment or mistake which proves fatal; and the final ending, in which nothing remains but the skeletons left on sand or rocks millions of miles away from their earth homeland. Like Jackie, many of the other narrators have lived in families in which the adults are continually determining on fresh starts or giving up after attempting one.

A space ship out in outer space
they got lost in space
they land on a planet and the space ship gets wrecked
they have to build another one from the parts
they fix it up and they're gonna take off
they put the rockets on
and everyone's in there it'll blow up
and it'll kill them because it was the wrong fuel
and they went up to heaven
and they dies
and there was just skeletons lying around on the sand underneath parts of the
    rocket.

48. Tragic Hero

by Sandy; eleven, who has the "black-sheep" role in a large, struggling family. He is a passive boy with the ideal of "relaxing", but his parents are both ill, and anxiously put pressure on him to do some work at home because his older brothers have job problems. Sandy has had remedial teaching since he was seven to try to teach him to read. He feels "stuck" and has begun truanting. In the story you can see characteristic delinquent attitudes—he was doing nothing, just standing there, and still you get into trouble; you try to help someone, you'll get in trouble, do anything you get in trouble, there's no escape anywhere—if the law doesn't kill you, the lawless will.

Just standing there
and he's watching these people having a fight
and police come along
and he arrested for nothing, just standing there,
and he gets in jail and can't come out,
and everyone say he guilty,
and he has to go to prison,
and say he killed someone
and he never because the other people kill him.

The man who got in jail went to help him,
and he died,
and the person saw him pick him up,
and he's to go to court, court case and all that,
and sentenced to death, life imprisonment.

Then he breaks out,
and then he goes to the island,
no one there watching for him,
and everyone looks for him and can't find him,
and he's alone on the island.
Natives there end up killing him,
and they kill him,
then they chop off his head because they're headhunters,
and then they stick his head and that.

THE WORLD IS A DISASTROUS PLACE

One of the earliest things that babies learn is their idea of whether the world is a good place or a bad place; whether life is to be trusted or mistrusted. As they grow older, new learning is assimilated into the attitudes they already have, and so new developments take place. Most of us learn that the world is both good and bad, that people are a mixture of good and bad, and it is necessary to know when to trust and when to mistrust. The stories of children often show their knowledge of this complexity.

However, when children have seen hopes dashed again and again, promises broken, love offered and taken away and parents making new relationships that always fail again sooner or later, they learn to become suspicious even of good things and good times. They know better. Cars are for crashing.

49. Crash

by Bruno, eight, another bully terrorising a school. Bruno had a severe speech defect, was overweight, and was strong enough to throw a desk the length of the classroom if asked to do schoolwork. He did not seem to care how many children he attacked at once. His migrant father beat him severely at home and was critical of his teachers for not doing the same at school. His mother was a frightened little thing, rarely seen out of the home, and even then always with her hair in curlers.

When Bruno was asked to draw and tell a story about anything he liked, he told this story of a plane crash; asked to make up a story about a person, he told about a boy crashing on a motor-bike; asked for the story he would like to have if he could have any story he liked, he told a story about a jet and a ship, both on fire.

They plane is on fire,
then they crash over the car,
and the driver be very lucky
e diden kill isself,
and all the people in the plane they killed,
lotta amblelan gotta come,
all d amblelan went down to the oppdelol,
lot of doctors got to come,
they have to dee if they are kill or not . . . some people are orright.

50. Plane Crash

by Pericles, seven. This is another characteristic plane crash story by "children who fail", this time by a neglected-looking shaggy-headed boy from a migrant family that has often been hit by unemployment and illness, and which has developed despondent expectations about the future. The family is difficult for any social agency to help, because all suggestions are bound to go wrong. If at last something seems to be succeeding, there will be almost morbid satisfaction when one or other of them can report back that something else has again spoilt their chances. In a story like Pericles', there is even relief with the final

and then they're dead. Full stop.

because then nothing else horrible can happen any more.

Children from happy backgrounds also enjoy telling stories about crashes, sometimes with relish about the gory melodrama—unlike the flat narration of these children—but often the interest centres on the initiative and courage of the heroes who save the day. Two of these "Real Adventure" stories are included on pp. 149–150 for comparison.

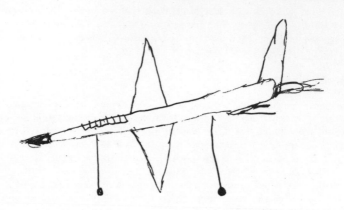

It's only about the aeroplane. They're going to smash.
It's gonna land, and the stair come and then the people come,
and then there's this truck, and they can put their bags and things in it,
and it goes in circles this thing, and then they get their bags and a taxi and
    go home
Once upon a time this aeroplane was going through the mountains with
    some people,
and they nearly wasted out of gas, and they only had half an hour to go,
and they might have a smash and the people might be injured and the
    drivers will be too,
and there are lions and all other animals and they might if they aren't dead
they might the animals might kill them. And then they're dead.
Full stop.
That's all.

51. The Cars Won't Stop

by Lisetta, seven, who has been battered. It is perhaps significant that when boys describe crashes, they identify with the people, planes, ships, cars that crash; girls are more likely to be the victims who are hit.

She's standing in the middle of the road.
She wants to stop the cars, but she can't.
The cars won't stop, and the cars will just run over her/
Then she'll have to go to the doctors, to the hospital.

It should already be apparent how little are children's imaginations restricted to their own physical environment and familiar childhood events. Here is another recurring theme in the stories of "disadvantaged" boys—the Sinking Ship. Very few of them have even been down to the docks a few miles away, some of them have never been in a rowing boat, probably none have ever seen a battleship or a ship in full sail like the ones they draw. But, like many boys everywhere, they like to draw ships.

But then, almost inevitably in their stories, the ships sink.

52. The Ship that Battled and Fighted for our Country

by Jim, seven. In Jim's story, it becomes very clear who and what the gallant little ship represents, as it fights against all odds. This ship was hit amidships by a cannonball. Jim had been in hospital because he had been battered with an iron bar by another bigger boy at the orphanage and left out in a paddock all night before he was found unconscious.

You might like this one.
The ship that I just drawed was a warship.
It battled and fighted for our country.
*   I forgot one thing.*
*   The ship sunk then.*

That's an Australian sign there.
Old cannon—it got a cannonball through there.

It was a brave ship.

53. The Boat Going Shailing

by Maurice, nine, whose family had already broken up several times, and who had already lived in two different children's institutions. Here Maurice is trying to believe that this time nothing will happen—the sky is blue. But shortly after this story was told Maurice's fears for the future were proved justified. Sure enough, the captain "was killed"—caught by the police this time—and Maurice was separated from his mother and brothers again.

The boat going shailing
and then some birds flying
and then it was blue sky.

And all the water got in the boat,
and it got all the men,
and some aeroplanes were coming down and they killed the captain,
and the boat sank.

54. The Rocket that Wouldn't Work

by Jeff, nine, a boy who has very quick enthusiasms, but gives up very easily. There may be some understanding of this when, as far as Jeff can see, effort is only postponing the inevitable tragedy. You haven't been given a decent working rocket for a start—fix it and get going, you get on fire—escape from the fire into the river—escape from drowning and the wild animals devour you. The nine-year-old boy has simply extended the range of disaster further than the seven-year-old Pericles (Story 50, p. 85).

A rocket. They're gonna go up to the moon—it—
The rocket wouldn't work.
They'll look at the engine and seen what was wrong
and they'd fixed it and then they got in the rocket and went up and when they
 got a big close to the moon, the rocket got on fire.
The people who was in the rocket jumped out of it, and they didn't have a
 parachute on,
and they fell in the river, and there was lizards, crocodiles, sharks in there
 too.

MODELS CHILDREN COPY

People always learn a great deal by imitation. Small children, especially, learn this way, but even more important for their whole lives is the sort of imitative learning called identification and introjection, in which, in a way, the most significant people in their early lives become part of their very selves. In a sense, we carry our parents around with us for good or ill.

Often the early hero-figure we have identified with is not any real person at all—but the way we have seen that person when we were young. This can be the child's first awareness of ideals and inspiration—but it can work the other way. The next stories all show the part a small boy's early identifications can play in the development of an anti-social and delinquent personality. The problem is particularly difficult when a boy identifies with a father that the mother hates.

55. Father and Son

by Raymond, nine. Again and again when a boy tells two stories together, one will be fantasy or adult life, and the other will be a companion-piece from a boy's life. (See also Story 38, p. 73). Here Raymond shows his identification with his father, who has job troubles as well as having a car that continually breaks down if it is not actually crashing. Dad has to get outside help; he can't make a go of things on his own. Raymond also has "crashes", and the symbolic "hospital" to repair the damage is his mother—the woman of the Australian matriduxy.

Drawing of a Car

My father can drive a car.
He smashes.
Then a tow-truck pulls him away.
The ambulance came and take him to hospital/
Then he gets a new car.

Drawing of a Boy

Someone might have bashed him up
and then he went home crying
and then his mother complained to his—to that boy
and then she told his mother
and then his mother gave him the strap.
    That's all.

Fathers appear significantly often in boys' stories. They are the comrades in play and work, the rivals, the models the sons will follow. Very often, Dads are depicted as stupid fools, highly accident prone. When they drive cars, they crash them; when they play football, they get injured. This marked lack of hero-worship is less often found among middle-class boys. The psycho-analytic picture of the boys' jealous rivalry is only supported explicitly in a small minority of stories—as in one eight-year-old boy's tale elaborating the TV epic of Deadly Ernest, in which the boy tells of being killed by a ghost that went to bed with his mother, but then the boy was resurrected and displaced the ghost. More common attitudes about fathers seem to be assimilated from the contempt shown them by their wives, plus overtones from the Dagwood-Flintstone-ridden culture which consistently depicts male parents as morons to laugh at.

Boys are in a particularly difficult situation when they cannot take pride publicly in their fathers, because their achievement or way of life are counter to community and school values. It is sometimes easier to hold up one's head when Dad is not there as evidence against you. One boy whose father is in jail told a long story about his heroism in Vietnam. A conflict of loyalties is shown in Brad's story about *My best thing*, because Brad's father was in jail too.

56. My Best Thing

by Brad, eight. Society hates Brad's father. His mother hates Brad's father. Brad is not supposed to know his father is in jail. Brad is loud in his denunciation of criminals and admiration for the police. But into his story there does creep some secret admiration for the criminal too; he cannot be completely disloyal. At school he is extremely violent, sensitive to the slightest word that may be directed to him.

I'll tell you my best thing.
My best thing be in a home and building buildings,
And after be a teacher, shopkeeper, policeman.
Policeman do very important jobs, they catch
criminals.
Got to be a real careful driver to catch criminals.

Some policemen have accidents.
A boy threw a stone at a policeman who was on the roof fixing things back
*   the boys had taken at the factory,*
And he fell off and taken to St Bridge's Hospital (St Vincent's),

Some criminals they can get caught.
Because some people go in the bank, steal money.
254 dollars we had stolen and policemen couldn't catch them.
Some criminals put them in secret hideouts way out in the country.

Brad's story shows some of the confusion when a boy's father causes him shame. Today when so many boys are fatherless, it is socially very important to know whether they can really do without them. Can sex-roles be so completely blurred that a boy can learn the sort of adult he can become from his mother, or a girl learn how to relate emotionally to people who are not women?

The next stories are by three boys who have made three different adjustments to being without fathers.

57. My Dad Doesn't Work for my Mum

by Jason, seven, who was expelled ("asked not to come back") from school (at seven!) because he became uncontrollable soon after his father finally left home. Jason's father had always been irresponsible and violent, but when he left the children idolised him, and were wildly excited when he occasionally reappeared with presents and promises. They had too little contact with him to remember him in disillusioning reality, while the remaining parent bore the disheartening burden of care and discipline against which the children rebelled. Now Jason's mother could not control Jason's violence and irresponsibility, and the little boy's dream was to be like the father whom she hated and downgraded.

My Dad gives me money, and he doesn't work for my Mum,
and he shifted from our house,
and my Mum was being mad at him.

I've met him at football, and he used to live with me.
Sometimes I sleep with my Dad.

58. The Werry Bad King

by Daryl, seven, who was a very nicely-behaved, conscientious little boy when he first arrived in a children's home, but in a few months had begun to copy the bigger boys in speech and swagger.

That's a king, was very rich,
and he was werry bad too (speech becoming more babyish)
and he used to steal things,
and he was a bad king.

And one day someone caught him stealing,
so he couldn't put him in the dungeon,
he escaped because he had the money what he steals in his pocket,
and he stealed again and again and again,
and one day there was army tanks out in the street one day, because there
   was a war,
war gonna start, and they bombed him and that was the end of the King,
the end for King Herod.

59. The Flasher Monkey

by Darren, ten. The psychological development of children of deliberately single
mothers is still not very clear, particularly how boys grow up when their mothers
are hostile to men. We have only the examples from other societies, such as the
American negro ghettos, or the histories of strong individual personalities in our
own. It is puzzling to wonder what sort of adult Darren will become—the boy who
told the story of *The flasher monkey* with its self-demeaning sexual undertones.
Darren's mother is openly contemptuous of men, and has a very poor opinion of
Darren himself, campaigning to have him put in a special school for the mentally
retarded. Since Darren also regarded himself as stupid and horrible, the teachers
also came to share his mother's opinion. In fact, he was of average intelligence.
His handicap was not intellectual.

Got a great big split in his trousers
There's his tail down the back.
This man was walking along,
and got a monkey in his shirt at the back,
and the monkey was making a hole in his trousers,
and the monkey wants to show his tail,
and puts his tail down,
and the man's walking around,
and the man comes over to him and says, "I didn't know you had a tail!"
and I said, "I haven't!"
and he said, "Look at the back of you, but you have got a tail!"
"Oh, that stupid monkey!"
And he took the monkey home and give him a smack to the backside when
   he got home.

It has often been observed that victims of oppression will side with their oppressors,
and when they get a chance will make others suffer as they suffered. Little boys who

are "bashed up" physically or psychologically will often tell stories of being destroyed; when they are older, they will be the destroyers—although in their stories even the aggressors are usually still the victims of fate. Warnings of consequences are little use to change these boys' behaviour. They expect disaster.

60. Making Like the Robot

by Tibor, six, who drew a spread-eagled stick-figure spiderman with blank eyes, holding a small car in one pronged finger of one hand, and a building like a bunch of sticks in the other. Tibor is terrorised at home by his father and uncles (as is his mother).

> *It's a big robot person.*
> *He's crunching up a little car.*
> *Now he's nipping a building.*
> *It's getting smaller.*
> *He's a big robot, a hundred years old,*
> *and he ends up crunched and all small,*
> *he's a big robot.*
> *Now I draw a boy.*

(He draws a milder version, with enormous blank eyes, and shorter arms and legs, and a tiny stick figure in one hand, instead of a car.)

> *He's a big boy with big eyes and small nose and little*
> *   mouth and short arms and one leg is long and the*
> *   other is short.*
> *His foot got chopped.*
> *It's a little baby. I show ya. Doing the same like the robot did,*
> *crunching up the building*
> *and the other hand crunching up a little boy.*
> *Dead/*
> *He ends up rusted. It's only a robot one.*
> *Rusted. See, all rusted. Tinny. He's rusted here*
> *And the building ends up smaller and smaller.*

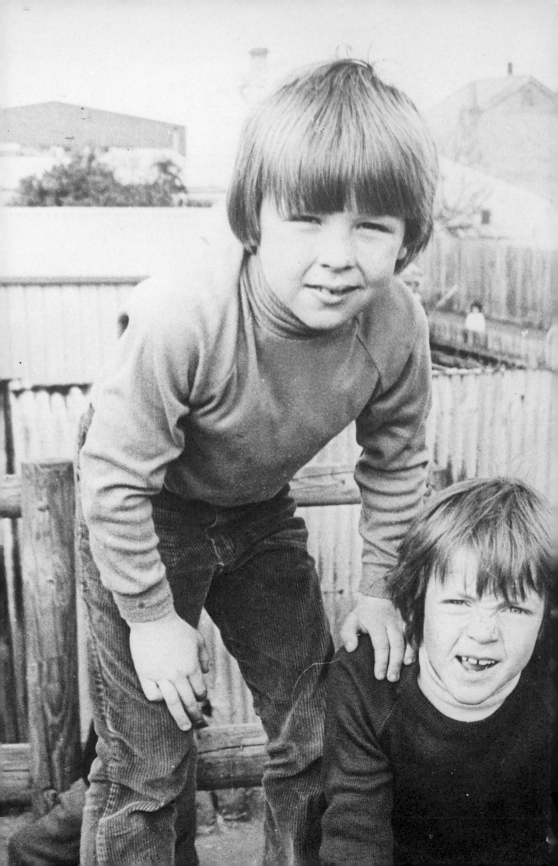

LOOKING FOR ESCAPE—THE RUNNING BOYS

There seems to be no generalisation possible about whether it is psychologically less damaging for children to live in a separated family rather than in one continually disrupted by parental disturbances. It may be a matter of sampling that this collection does not include any stories by happy children from broken homes, but there are many among them that suggest that both physical and psychological disruption can cause children intense anxiety and misery, and that the psychological disturbance caused when parents "fight and yell" may not stop with what parents call "a clean break" but can continue—much as it possibly continues in the parents' minds too.

Even after a family has lived apart for years, children may tell stories full of the incomprehensible events leading up to and around the break—as in the story *Far far far far far far far away*, below—including stories in which the child reveals his belief that he himself is the guilty though innocent cause of the disaster, or, very often, is the only one really aware of what is happening, and tries to stop the tragedy in vain. (e.g. Story, 32 p. 65)

Sacco, the six-year-old boy who told the next story, was one of the reasons for my producing this book, with its plea that we should be able to spare children these destructive experiences. He was one of three children of a migrant family that had been deserted the year before by their violent, heavy-drinking, irresponsible father, leaving a bitter and anxious mother who saw repeated in her little son everything that she hated most in her husband, and, as the story shows, leaving a boy who cannot come to terms with the past, nor with his mother's unhappiness.

At school Sacco was rapidly becoming uncontrollable, although he was still friendly and delightful, and casual observers would be struck by his apparent bubbling happiness and spontaneity. Soon, however, his teachers would learn how quickly his moods changed. They described him as "a bee in a bottle", who could learn nothing at all in school because he could not keep still or attend at all. In his story, Sacco himself described what seem like his own unsuccessful attempts to reduce his frenzied and goal-less activity:

. . . . and then he stopped down.
And then he stopped and then he slowed down and he slowed down
and he couldn't slow and he couldn't slow and
he couldn't and couldn't
and then he did and did and he did,
and then he couldn't stop and still going (racing)
still   still   still
and then he went far far far far far far far far far far far far far far far far
    far far far away . . .

Sacco is one of the inner suburbs' Running Boys trying to escape the intolerable— but they have nowhere to escape to, and nothing to stop their continual running, or to pacify the terrifying predatory animals who symbolise their emotional lives. There are comparable figures in Greek legend, driven before the Furies—or the tales of the Flying Dutchman, or the Wandering Jew, or adult vagrants over the face of the earth. But Sacco was only six.

61. Far far far far far far far away

by Sacco, six.

He's walking in a sunny day,
he's gotta do shopping.
Then the policeman will come and pick him up because he says a bad word,
then he'll go in jail,
then he'll get killed,
then he have to go to hospital,
then he have to stay there for a long long time,
then he'll be dead,
then he won't be able to come out.

Then he'll start crying, then he'll stop crying, then he'll say to the doctors,
  "Help me."
Then he'll say, "Please can you help?"
Then he'll start crying.
Then he'll start being sad,
then he'll start to call his Mum,
He'll say, "Mother! Mother!"
Then he . . . then he'll go to sleep.
Then the doctor will give him medicine to go home,
and then he'll be home.
Then he'll go home and say Hullo to his Mother,
and his Mum starts crying.
And he say, "It's a rainy day."
Then he'll say, "Pity need a umbrella,"
Then he hid it out and got wet hair,
then he goes to the toilet, then he gets his hands wet, then he dries them,
and then he gets em wet again,
and then he leaves them wet.

Then he gets his bag and go away and lives somewhere else.
And then he goes to fix his Mother up.
Then he goes to be naughty,
he'll go to whack his mother,
and then he'll go and muck around and fight his mother,
and then she'll have to go up to the hospital,
and then she'll get a needle,
and then his father went to see her and then he went to get her up for a
   long walk,
and he had a car, and then he drived there,
and then he went to see and she was spewing,
and she was spewing sick
and she starts going to sleep.
And she went to sleep, fast, fast asleep,
and she woke up and screamed.
And then she woke up and said Hullo to his father,
and then the whole family went home
and they lived all together,
and then they said they weren't to go in, so they did
and then they went out yesterday and they had a happy day,
and then they washed their hands when they got home,
and then they got everything and shifted,
then his mother came home,
and then he run away.
And then his Mother run away with him,
and then the fox came and eat them up,
and the fox et em up.
and then the fox started to go home,
and then the people never lived ever again.
And then he went everywhere he liked to go,
and then they lived happy together then that was all.

Then they said, "It's nearly finished."
And then they said, "There's a tiger!"
and then they all run away.
And then they said, "We'll run away now,
We'll find another space."
And then the mother came with him,
She said, she'll find another space with him.
Then she got it back and got all her clothes all packed up,
then she started to cry.
Then his father started to cry,

and then was she said, that was the end,
and his father said, "It's NOT the end."

And then he run far far far away,
and his Mother followed him,
and then his Mum run back to her own house,
and she shouldn't couldn't get there,
cos the tiger was there.
Then she run back, then she said, "Father! Father! Father!"
Then she said, "Father, father!"

And that was the story of the old man junkie.
Then he run down the stairs and run far far away,
and then he went then he stopped down,
and then he was standing there, and then he couldn't get past,
and then he went far far far far far far far away,
and then he stopped right there.
Then he turned a corner and then he saw a tiger.
Then he saw another monkey.
Then he saw all the all anibles,
then he stopped there and he slept there.
Then he so cried, and then he dropped dead.
Then he saw this thing, and he picked it up and he looked in it,
and he said, "What are you looking in that?" then the policeman came.
And then he said, "Gimme my biro back!"
And then he said, "Can you put my leg back on?"
And then I can't say no more, what can I say?

It was a lady there with him, and there was another man,
and then he drawed a little man,
only piece of paper,
and he ripped it and throwed it away,
and then he stopped—shouldn't throw that away,
and then he started to cry for a long long long long long long long long long
*   long long long time,*
and then he stopped crying and he ran far far far away,

and then he went far far far far far far far far far far far far far far far
*   far far far away,*

and then he stopped at the end.
And then he went back to his place, and that was far far far far far far
*   far far far far far far far far far far away,*
and then he stopped right on there, where all the tigers was,

and then he went far far far way to the trees, and he stayed there for a long
    long long long long long long time,
and he couldn't get past for a long long long long long long long long long
    long long time
then he got past because the gate opened,
and then he had to run far far far far far far far far far far far far far far
    far far far far far far far far far far far far far far far far far far
    far far away,
and he couldn't get past, then he got past and then he run far far far far
    far far far far far far far far away
and then he seen all the tigers and they all all all all all all run run run run
    run run all around the place.
Then he stopped there.
Then he went far far far and far away.
Then he stopped right at the end of the gate, and then went right up to the
    end of . . right up to the end.
Then he said, "Can you let me past, please?" the big big big . . .
and then he saw a Giant, then he saw a long long long long long long long
    long long long long long long Giant,
and then he ran far far far far far far far far far far far far far far far far
    far far far far far far far far far far far far far far far far far far
    far far far far far away.
And then he said, "What are you doing here?" and then that was the end.
And then he went far far far far far far far far far far far far far far far far
    far away, and then he stopped at the end.
And then he said, "What are you doing here?"
And then he said, "Can you come with me, please please please please
    please?"
And then he stopped talking and then he went, "Come, come come come
    come come come come come come come come come come come come,"
And then he stopped and then he went walk alk alk alk alk alk,
and then he run far far far far far far far far far far far far far far away
    away way,
and then he saw all animals that were in this street far far away,
and then he could get there, because all the animals around there,
and then he stopped there and then he slowed down,
and then he went far far far far way, because he could get past all them
    animals and animals and animals—can't remember—
and then all the trees blown.

And then he stopped down,
and then he were far far far far away,

and then he went far far far far far far far away, and far far far far far
*   far far far far far far far far far far far far far far far far far far far*
*   far far far far far far away,*
and then he stopped down.
And then he stopped and then he slowed down and he slowed down and he
*   couldn't slow and he couldn't slow and he couldn't and couldn't*
and then he did and did and he did,
and then he couldn't stop and still going (racing)
*   still   still   still*
and then he went far far far far far far far far far far far far far far far
*   far far far away*
and then he went right over there to Sydney and then he stopped there,
and then he went right over there and stopped where he was and then he
*   went out to play for a long long long long long long long time,*
and then he went right over there and fell down the bridge,
right right right down the bridge,
and then he couldn't get back up,
and he shried and he shried and he tried and he tried tried tried tried
and then he stopped right down the bridge.
And then he said, "There's tigers over there!"
and then he ran far far far far far far far far far far far far far far far
*   far away,*
and then he stopped right where he was and then he went right down the
*   hill right right right down the hill,*
and then he stopped and stopped and stopped stopped stopped stopped
*   stopped stopped.*
and then it is the end of the story, and then he went right down that hill,
*   very very very down the hill and then he stopped right down to the end,*
and then he went right down there
and then he went right down the hill and up and right to there,
and he stopped over here near the end,
and then he said, "I want to go somewhere, I want to go somewhere,"
and then he went there,
and then he went far far far far far far far far far far far far far far away,
and then he stopped right at the end.

62. The Dangerous Picture

by Sacco's sister Marietta, nine, a dear, quiet little girl, "so different from Sacco", except that, like him, she still cannot read or write because she keeps mixing up the letters, writing back to front, and forgetting how to do sums. But it is clear from the story that although her mother sees Marietta as her shield and support in bringing up the two younger children, the child is also affected by the bitterness and hardship.

In the story's illustration, the fire was represented by scribbles that became faster and fiercer and eventually covered the picture.

He's chopping the house down right—dirt, no door there,
and here's all the fire coming,
he's chopping that, and there's all smoke coming up,
because it's all old, and there's all little boys in there,
and it's all scribble on the walls and they got chopped out,
and they're the flats, and they got fire, they's got all
*   fire over the flowers and the little boy,*
looking at all the fire coming, and that's that—
it's a dangerous picture.

Cos when they got chucked out, they went and lit a fire in the house,
and they didn't have nowhere to live,
and then—was all running away, and all little apples falling over the
*   tree,*
all of them, all over the place,
and the man got all burnt up—
—oh, gee, there's a lot of fire!

Here's more fire coming up on the flowers.

63. Running Away

by Adam, eight. It would be interesting to know what the reader could learn about Adam from this story alone. His deserting father periodically reappears for brief and upsetting intervals, his mother is ailing and irritable, and he is failing at school. He does not truant, but he would like to. The story describes his mixed-up attitudes and interprets his real-life unpredictable and inconsistent behaviour, as well as his mother's. Every phrase here seems a relevant and meaningful symbol.

I'll draw a man—not good at his face. This bit's the hardest. (feet)
I'll put him wearing braces—that's the little clip.
He looks like flattened down by the steam-roller.
He's walking down the street and he drops some money,
the five cents, and the highest bill, twenty dollars.
He doesn't know, does he!
And he kicks up mud over the money.
And he looks in his pockets there,
and can't find and says to his mother, "I'd better go and look for it,"
and he slips in the mud,
and the money goes up and lands on his head.
And he tells his mother the truth
and didn't get into trouble.

And mother says, "What's on your head?"
and he said, "I didn't think."
"Here, and there's twenty dollars and five cents!"
And he says, "Sorry, sorry."
"You better not come in this house,"—cos she's real mad,
"Work for twenty dollars and got mud all over it!"

And he had never had a good dinner in his life,
for that thing—it starts with "r"—run away.
He feel happy because he run away,
because he took fourteen dollars with him.
He said he will spend on food, not those rubbish lollies.
The next day he's out of food, because he bought lollies.
The next day he goes home and steals the purse and says a
    rude word to his mother,
then he runs away and burns up the house.
And the fire brigade come,
and get the police and it gets into the paper and the boy into jail.

Just because of one little accident, the money from his pocket,
the house got burnt down.

He want to play cricket by himself—
the spade, bucket, ball . . .
He dug and dug and dug, and they said, "Come back!"
and he dug himself out in the desert,
and a camel came by and walked on his head.
It didn't see him when the camel went by. He said, "Look up, mister."
Hoo! There's a lot there!
Happy, I'll make it end happy.

He went home and said sorry and his mother got mad and he went to
the police and told them the completely truth.
His mother got a fever and died and he went to the police and told
them everything and the policeman gave him a happy home.
The end.

64. Running in the Night

by Chris, eight, failing and confused at school, and confused by parental behaviour at home too. This boy's panic is less than that so apparent in Stories 12 and 14 (pp. 40 and 41). He is no longer terrified by ghosts like the little boy who cannot understand the frightening things of the world, nor chased by persecutors. He starts off "walking not running" but he is still driven to escape . . . something, which seems to be connected with the insecurity of unexplained events, adult secrets, adult mistrusting and adult mixed emotions.

The boy lived down here, but he went down there,
so he turned wrong way to get to the school,
the boy didn't know how to cross, all the footpath.

The boy came back, and the mother said, "You're late,"
and the mother gave the boy a smack.
He lived in the street, walking not running.
He left 9 o'clock, and he was late,
and come back home at four o'clock,
and he tried when it was in the night,
he sneaked out the window,
and ran out,
and when light turned red, he ran out across the road,
and the mother was looking for the boy,
and the mother forgot he went home yesterday,
and the mother went down the school,
and the mother found the boy.

The boy felt sorry for the mother.
He was going to go home, so the mother went straight away.
The father didn't come home till two days,
because he had two stitches in his head,
because crashed it in his car, with a great big rock.

The mother didn't even know,
because the father didn't tell the mother,
because the father didn't want to,
and then the mother would hate the father,
because she'd wonder why he'd have stitches,
because she don't care if they had crashed.

When they take the stitches out, it still goes open again,
he just goes to bed and waits till he gets fixed up by the doctor.
The boy just cared.
And when he cared, well, in the night time, again he ran out. |

The boy didn't like the mother, because the mother didn't let the boy play
*   in school where all the playmates coming out.*

65. Zabriskie Point

by Desmond, sixteen, an English boy up before the courts for stealing and drug-pushing—although not an addict himself. "The story you would like to have" is his account of a film he has seen, and shows the philosophies he uses to justify anything he wants to do. He is much more hostile about his family than the objective facts would explain, although his father "has always felt there was something bad in him".

It's Zabriskie Point.
About a bloke, a student, going to his . . . on probation.
Police are after him for stealing—for getting an aeroplane.
Nicked an aeroplane, flying around in it.
Film tried to show you what America's like, the corruption, how false, all
*   the advertising . . .*
He's always flying around and enjoying himself. He hasn't nicked it, it's
*   just to enjoy himself, not to keep it always. Girl with him.*
He brings the aeroplane back, they're all on patrol and the police caught
*   him.*
And when he gives it back, they just shot him.

CALLING FOR HELP

Many of the stories in this book have two very significant features—the characters in them cannot save themselves, nor is there any source of help they can hope for.

However, "Calling for Help" stories are also common, and again it is significant what sort of help is called for. It is usually to be mended, or even remade. The children turn for help to agencies—police, hospitals, ambulances, rather than to parents or other individuals.

66. The Robot Screaming Out for Help

by Janella, eight, referred for psychiatric help because her mother said that she was uncontrollable. When Janella was asked to draw anything she liked, she played safe, and drew a plain table and chair—but when asked to tell a story about it, the feelings inside her overcame her control, and she told this story of a "human" machine at the mercy of persecution by real people, and without a real machine's protection of being unable to suffer. It is as if she did not feel really part of humankind herself, and yet people were like enemies that got within as well as without. The robot screams with anger and helplessness at their callousness—and in her story the people are merciful. In some children's stories, however, the help does not come, and the enemy keeps on laughing.

But I can make it into something else. A robot.
They're buttons. (?) Just smiling.
(?) He's blowed up, going to be blowed up,
cos this aeroplane up here blowed him up.
There's a parachute, that comes out of that aeroplane,
and going down there and just by the rocks,
and laughing at him because he's being blowed up
and there's people kind of inside him/

They make friends with him.
They decide not to blow him up any more
because he was screaming out for help—
can't write it down there— (in a black balloon)
because he was screaming out for help.

67. Getting Mended

by Zlotko, eleven, who cannot read despite average intelligence and years of remedial help. There is some evidence that his first schooling was a "sink or swim" experience in a crowded school with teachers who emphasised that children should learn for themselves, without teaching. Zlotko did not learn for himself, and he sank. It is reasonable for a helpless eight-year-old to depend on adults for help, and even scream for it, like Janella (p. 109) but Zlotko has such a poor opinion of himself and his abilities to do anything for himself, that he is looking for someone to remake him, so that he can be a superman—and *then* he can do marvellous and kind things. And he looks to the hospital to do all these necessary transplants.

Zlotko as an adult may still be very much the same. So many adults, too, think they could make a go of their lives if they were turned into different people by some agency. So many of them turn to social agencies and doctors for help—"they" should solve all the problems.

Zlotko can also be seen as desiring to become a sort of robot, rather than a person, and there are undertones that he could exploit the power this gave him, punishing as well as helping.

In a racing track and going round a corner
and then he crashes
and then another bloke crashes,
and have to bring in to the hospital.

Then he gets
two new arms, two new legs and a new eye, then he got a real good eye,
    got an eye cross so he can spot more things more good,
and got new legs made out of metally, real strong,
can run faster than anybody else,
got two new strong arms, strong as bulldozers.

And then he starts helping those blokes,
then these other blokes come along and starting trouble,
and this man has to go put them in jail,
and gets them puts them in jail,
and then he . . . it's not very good . . . /

He ends up helping all the good people
and gets rid of all the bad.

III What Happens...

The child is father of the man

Wordsworth

When the baby lions grow up,
"they go hunting to kill people"

Stephen, Story 89

The stories of suburban children tend, on the whole, to be optimistic in outcome, but the stories of children with "disadvantaged" backgrounds tend, on the whole, to be pessimistic.

Only longitudinal studies as children grow up can answer the question about whether these expectations are themselves self-fulfilling prophecies, which could help us to understand the vicious cycle of "psychological poverty" which often seems to go round from one generation to the next.

We could follow up in real life whether children who see themselves as successful and competent in their fantasy lives will also become competent in their adult lives. Is it significant that they see the solutions to the crises in their stories to lie in the acts of their heroes, who are able to do something about their predicaments, and are not crushed by disaster? How self-sufficient will be the children who turn their heroes over to ambulances, hospitals and even policemen for succour—after the damage is done and often too late?

Adults may be partly to blame for passing on fatalistic attitudes—that the individual is helpless, or that what ends happily is unrealistic and sentimental. Even teachers will say, "Well, that is real life, isn't it?" when commenting on a children's reader showing a home in which every action by father or child is an accident, breakage or spillage—as if blind to the fact that most of the time that is not real life.

For children with bad experiences of the world, the basic attitudes of adults to the world may be perceived as depression and anger. This holds for both men and women, but what is usually most apparent in the way these feelings are manifested is the woman as victim, the man as aggressor. In the next two stories, by Marietta and Mahmoud, that man and that woman exist already in the children.

68. The Girl with Blonde Hair

by Marietta, eight, a migrant child from a home where all the breadwinners are sick and unemployed. Marietta's mixed-up feelings come through clearly—what she wishes and what she fears, almost in alternate sentences. The wishes are that the girl is happy, she has blonde hair (many dark-complexioned migrant children describe blonde heroines and princesses in their stories), she is tall, she has lots of jewellery and a nice baby, and she goes to the shop. But like a theme in a fugue the fears keep breaking in—the girl gets smacked, she isn't tall, she's short, she gets eaten by the Wolf, she has no shoes, her sister is eaten by the Wolf, and then the other sister is eaten too.

The girl is happy
The little girl yesterday had gotten the smacks
Are you writing the sentence down?
The girl has blonde hair
her eyes are blue
she is a nice girl and she is tall—
no she isn't, she is short!
and if she goes out to the park
the Big Bad Wolf will eat her
the little girl has lots of jewellery
and now she is eaten of the Big Bad Wolf.

The little girl is holding a baby is nice and she is sleeping
the girl has no shoes on
her mother—no—yes—her mother told her one day to go to the shop.
Her little sister had been ate by the Big Bad Wolf
now she has only one little sister left
and one day she had been ate from the Big Bad Wolf too.

69. The Victim Hits Back

by Mahmoud, nine, from an Egyptian family "down on its luck" and with one trouble following another ever since arrival in Australia. At school, Mahmoud was a "nice quiet little boy" with great dark eyes, who was referred because he was not learning anything. He just sat and looked around him, and wrote in his book only if someone sat next to him, constantly "encouraging" him. Then, when asked to draw anything he liked and tell me a story about it, Mahmoud drew a long figure, all limp outline with no features, and told this story about the man who murdered and stole, and ran away and called for help, escaping into an orgy of revenge.

He's killing a man,
the cops saw him
and he runned away
and said, "Help!"
keeps on running,
stealed its diamonds
and he killed a lady
and he killedet a boy, and he killedet a girl, and
*   he killedet a man, and he killedet a cops, and*
*   he killedet a dog, and he killedet a cat,*
killed
he broke the shop down,
stealedet the car, stealed the car the tyres,
and he stealedet a car and he runned away with it,
and he smashed it in a man and keeps on running
killed another man
killed another lady
killed another girl.
Nothing else

Mahmoud's other drawing was of a very hungry dog that looks in dustbins for food and is killed for stealing.

WHEN I GROW UP

Young children are often asked what they want to be when they grow up, and their answers are often unrealistic. The commonest response for these children may be possibly, however—"a policeman", or "a robber or a policeman". A little boy of seven refusing to learn to read may see no reason for learning, since when he grows up he is going to watch television all day, and when he needs money, he will go out and rob a bank, and do it so someone else gets the blame and is put in jail, while he watches television until he needs more money. And he can explain in precise and convincing detail exactly how to rob a bank and divert suspicion on to someone else.

The first stories here are all by children with reputations as thieves already, then there is one by "the boy who gets away", and then two which illustrate what many boys already see as the alternative to an exciting, if doomed, life of crime. The honest job seems pretty doomed too.

70. "The Runbore"

by Garry, twelve, who is failing and truanting from school, and has already been caught stealing several times. Garry drew a picture of a lanky figure with blank eyes and no hair or clothing, and labelled it *the RUNBORE*

> *First, he's a robber, and a fat one at that,*
> *Got lots of hair*
> *Got a mask on*
> *He's smiling*
> *He hasn't got very long arms*
> *He's no good at robbing*
>
> *That's all, he's been caught hundreds of times*
> *He'll be in prison again/*
>
> *He robs to get money*
> *Because he's a very poor man*
> *He gets rich and never gets caught again*
> *and he takes off his mask*
>
> *He's a Chinese man.*

71. The Crook

by Dmitri, nine, who is a skinny undersized little migrant boy with a large head, which makes him look odd, although he is not really as stupid as he looks. Dmitri stole from cars, shops, and, it was thought, houses. He kept a hostile attitude to other children and was defensive against adults. Teachers thought that home conditions varied from harsh to chaotic.

Dmitri's figure of a person was distorted, with a long extended claw.

> *This man is sort of big, and he's got big eyes and a tongue,*
> *Look at his finger!*
> *He's going to get a woman and scratch her!*

This man is a crook, and he was hit at the shoulder,
and he felled on the policeman.
and he got a knife and killed him at the back/

And a couple of other policemen caught him and shot him.

Can I draw his woman too?

Can I make another one up?

72. The Burgular

by Mary Lou, nine, from a broken home, whose outbursts of petty thieving and violent anger recurred periodically, despite intervals of earnest resolution, almost like some sort of addiction.

She drew a house with a ruler, and the set of her mind seems shown when she asked, on beginning her story, "Do I have to do someone burglaring it?"

Do I have to do someone burglaring it? ("No"—and why should she?)
There was this man . . .
There were two people living in this house,
they went out Friday night shopping,
and there was this man—watching them day and night till they went out,
and this night he seen them going out and he said, "Right!
Now I'll begin going in to steal something."
And he got in the window,
and he looked everywhere, and behind this map of Australia he found the
* safe,*
and it had on the back of the map, "two hundred left, five hundred right,
* and sixty left",*

and he turned them numbers, and he found that there was no money in it,
only packets of cigarettes.

And one hour later, he went into this lady's drawer,
  and found thousands and thousands of dollars' worth of jewellery,
and then he said, "Righty-o, this is the place I am going to do the next
  round too."
And the lady found out,
and about nine o'clock she came and said, (squeaky voice)
"Oh, all my jewellery's been stolen"
and the man rung the police and the police came down and the police said,
"Can you give a description of what was stolen?" and the lady give the
  description,
and seven days later the police found the man, and he got five—twenty-five
  years in prison.
The end.

73. The Silly Sheriff

by Josef, twelve. Boys whose primary fantasy includes punishment and disaster are
often found out in their delinquencies, and adults who comment "You asked for it,"
may be right. What of the boys who do not get caught?

This story is by a pleasant-spoken twelve-year-old migrant boy with alert, wary
eyes. He does not fail at school. He does not get into trouble—because nothing
can be pinned on him. The police cannot *prove* that he burnt down the school.

The drawing about which Josef told his story was of a deceptively harmless-looking
"sheriff", with gun at the ready and a skull and crossbones on his hat.

*That's kind of a sheriff here, coming in a pub and there's all the people
    drinking.*
*And he's acting tough—the New Sheriff—so all the people be scared of
    him.*
And then nobody takes notice, and don't care about him.
He comes in and sees the drinking, and starts fighting with them,
And they pick him up and throw him out the window.
*Then he comes back and puts them under arrest and puts them in the office,
    and locks them up in jail again.*
Then they get away again.
He put a reward, but no-one couldn't catch them.
And then he forgot all about them.

Unfortunately there was no opportunity for Josef to tell a story about his other
drawing of "a person"—a strange and meticulous drawing of Tarzan in the jungle
with snakes and other familiars, a fearless primitive man, outside the laws of society
and backed by the dangerous denizens of the jungle. Josef took an hour to do all the
fine detail.

Boys often tell stories about adult ambitions, and achievements and adventures as men. Inner-urban migrant boys who are managing to succeed at school are often particularly determined to succeed, and tell stories about champion boxers and wrestlers, or rich peasant farmers, or great doctors. Sometimes these ambitions are hopeless, but often these boys do win through to something of what they want.

However, children failing at school, or surrounded by adult examples of disillusion or failure, may view the adult world of work as only another scene for failure or tedium. Zlotko (Story 67, p. 110) told a story about a man who worked a bulldozer on a rubbish dump, went home to sleep, have his tea, go to sleep, get up, work—but the best of it all was the sleeping. Others foresee a series of jobs, and making a mess of all of them.

74. The Disillusioned Cookaman

by Hertel, twelve, who wrote a story underneath his picture of a hotel cook:

This is a cookaman. This man work in a HOTel
called—   . He cook dinner every day.
And one day he said to him self. I will
kurck this work. This is the end.

This is what Hertel said about the picture:

Cookaman.
He's a cookaman, cook the dinner, work in a hotel.
Make it for the people.
Go home.
Ever day come to work here.
One day
He went to get another work,
Don't want to work any more here.

75. Non-Starter

by Angelo, thirteen, an Australian-born Italian boy who can barely read a first-grade primer. Note that "relax" is one of the early words in Australian children's vocabulary. ("Attack" is another.)

This boy's a student, and he's gonna school to learn,
He's gonna learn how to write,
and he'll get a job,
he'll get married,
he'll get kids,
he'll get a divorce,
he'll get another wife,
get married,
gets kids.

(?) Oh, they grow up by their mother.
(?) Nothing, he's not worried. (Like his job?)
No, he just wants to sit home and relax.

REVENGE ON THE UNIVERSE

The two most dominant emotions in the stories told by violent children are anger and depression. We can see what has happened to the children and inside the children to make them feel like this. The next series of stories illustrates what the children do with their anger.

What becomes very clear is that their anger does not dissipate by being expressed, whether in fantasy or in action—rather, violence breeds violence. The most violent children are the ones with the most obsessions about violence in their stories, and like the Running Boys unable to find anywhere to stop running (p. 97), the violent children are unable to stop their anger once it explodes. The only possible outcome and end to it is through fatal disaster. Unhappy children's rage extends beyond themselves and becomes cosmic, destroying if possible the whole universe which is ranged against them. In doing this very often they are only copying what seems to them the evil that terrorised them when they were young and helpless.

Criminals have sometimes been observed to have feelings of omnipotence—and this too can be seen in some angry children—but it is omnipotence for suicidal destruction. What penal sanctions can have effect on them when they hate themselves too?

These stories show the extension of hate, from the children whose blind anger is directed only to the destruction of their families, to those who would topple the cosmos with them.

76. Someone is Busting up the House

by Craig, six. When children tell stories about houses being on fire or smashed up, they may be expressing their own transient or long-lasting feelings of anger out of control, or their insecurity when parents are destroying the home. In this instance, Craig had been referred because he was being extremely violent and destructive at home—at a time when his father was threatening to leave home "but of course the children don't know about it". There is a strong likelihood that Craig is only acting out what his parents are actually doing.

A house, with a bedroom in the middle, the door's on that side.
That's us in it.

Our window's gonna get busted.
Someone was being banging on it.
Someone gonna be naughty.
Someone gonna bang the walls.
Someone will burst the doors/
Then the doors and windows will fall off.

77. They'll Cry for Me when I'm Dead

by Michelle, five. Most of us have probably felt like this at some time in our lives— that "nobody-loves-me-everybody-hates-me" feeling expressed in extravagant, hysterical, self-pitying terms. It is possible then for us all to imagine what it must be like to be a five-year-old whose parents constantly tell her she is a bad, horrible child, not like the rest of the family. This brief but characteristic outburst expresses the range of panic, despair, self-pity, anger, revenge and hopelessness that a small child can feel.

A girl named Michelle.
A dog's chasing her and he eats her all up.
She's gone.
The mother's crying for her . . .

Her sister's going to cry too.
Her mother's gonna cry.
The Dad cries.
The wolf eats the Mum up.
She's gone.
She's lying in the mud because the dog put her in the mud.
The Dad's eaten up.
The girl's dead.
The other sister is too, and the other brother's dead.
I don't know anything else.

78. The Firing Squad

by Derry, twelve. Derry is an isolate, with no friends at school, and no caring relatives. The stories of quite happy children are still likely to express the difficulties they feel in making and keeping friendships, and how important friendship is for them. From children's stories, it is apparent that for them the playground is far more important than the classroom. Yet in almost every school there are some children who seem to have no friends at all. Few of them "don't care", whatever disregard they may pretend. Their tragedy is that their very disability in making relationships with other children cuts them off from chances of ever learning how to.

Friendlessness has an appalling effect on children's self-image. How can you accept yourself if no one else will? Their resentment and hopelessness make them even more unattractive.

Derry's story is "the story you would like to have if you could have any story you liked". He is a pest, he is persecuted. But he imagines a posthumous revenge, completely imaginary, carried out by the friends who do not exist. He has no one on his side.

This man he was in the war
and got captured for shooting a man on the other side
men on the other side caught him
and so they captured him
and put him in a prison that they had
and he's been staying there a lot by himself
and he's being a pest and they want to get him out of the way
so they take him out to the firing squad,
the firing squad shoot him down
and he dies—

just a bit more—
so the men on his side find out
so they get all the men
and the men get all the weapons
and had a war against the other side and they win
and the other side was killed from all the bullets.

79. "The Teror" and The Mad Cowboy

by Kevin, eleven, a boy who seems to have no self-control either in real life or fantasy. He was so disruptive at school that he was given the label "Behaviour Disorder" and hardly seen as a human child at all. Although his first story was about a hot-rod, drawn like a large bug with wheels, pipes and antenna, and labelled THE TEROR, the description was apt for Kevin himself on a rampage. Kevin himself seems to expect that he will "blow up" one day in a final catastrophe, and is almost trying to provoke the inevitable end sooner.

When after that, Kevin was asked to tell a story about a person, he translated his first story into human terms, and the two narratives can be put side by side to compare their sequence. The cowboy feels himself to be mad, to begin with; when someone takes what he values, a Dr Jekyll change begins to occur, and the cowboy becomes a murderous personality, unable to tolerate anything from anyone.

THE TEROR

"The Teror"

What did happen? Crashed through the fence,
was heading for a building,
ran up a tree and went down again,
when it went down it jumped like a kangaroo,
landed on top of the building,
went right through the building to the bottom,
kept on going right up to the grandstand,
ran all over the people.
Then it ran out of fuel,
went back over the people again,
then it stopped/
After a little while, the car blew up.

The Mad Cowboy

He's mad. He got big shoes on.
He's a cowboy. Someone took his gun, he ran after him and got it . . .
After a while his hair started to curl, really curly,
his fingers began to grow longer.
He saw a boy jump down a hole, so went after him,
finally got his gun back, and shot him.
Grabbed all his jewels and took them back to the camp . . .
The captain said, "What big ears you got,
what curly hair,
what long fingers
what big boots."
and he looked mad.
And the cowboy said, "How dare you call me that!"
He got madder,
turned the gun barrel round,
shot him.

80. Homicide

by Romolo, seven. Romolo was referred because he was a new boy still not settled into Grade I after a month, having arrived in the middle of the term. He would speak to no one, and co-operated in nothing. The teachers did not know what to do with him.

Romolo drew me a picture of a rather primitive human being, mostly fingers and legs, and with no features. After some silence, this story came out, very flatly, even including the low growl of the machine gun.

It was Romolo's third new school in two years. His parents spoke no English at all, and Romolo was already acting as if he could not speak or understand their language.

He's doing with gun,

rrrrrrrrrrrrrrrrr!! rrrrrrrrrrrrrrrrrrrrr!
He wants to kill a man
because he's a man who kill all mans.

He's going to die.

81. The Man Who Wanted the Plane to Crash

by Noelene, eleven. Noelene was the handicapped twin of a bright, popular brother. She was a grade behind, always compared with him, and she thought herself ugly. She refused to play with girls and was a violent tomboy, although not associating with her brother. Her stories were all of men with violent ends, with masculine settings, as in this plane crash story. Unlike a boy's story, however, are the concern with feelings and motives and the cavalier attitude to factual detail.

As in the story of *The mad cowboy* (Story 79, p. 123) the anti-hero is trigger-sensitive to the slightest insult, there is something wrong with him—he is a bit mad—and his emotions are conflicting and unstable. He causes the crash, he calls the ambulance, he gets out of jail through good behaviour, he goes robbing banks, his brother is a highly ambivalent figure. Stealing, like the plane crash, represents revenge.

Noelene's picture of a boy and a girl.

> *There was this aeroplane and it was Ansett and it hold 160 passengers*
> *and they ran out of petrol and water and that and they all put on their*
>   *parachute and didn't do them no good,*
> *smashed into a tree and they all died,*
> *and it was someone's fault, because he got the oil and threw it out the*
>   *window, and went to prison for ten years,*
> *and it was a little boy, no, it is a man, he is twenty years,*
> *and he did it because he wanted it to crash*
> *because everyone got on his nerves in the bus because they said, "Are you*
>   *Italian?"*
> *and it landed near a lot of trees,*
> *and the man that done it called for a ambulance because they were all hurt,*
> *five bodies on the plane, all died.*
> *Didn't know what to do about the rest of them and rang a ambulance,*
> *twenty ambulances came because there were a lot of people,*
> *sixty of them died and the rest were all right.*

Then he went to jail and then got out through good behaviour,
then he died because he had something wrong with hisself,
he was a bit . . . mad
and he (inaudible) everything to him,
and he went on the plane because he wanted to go on a holiday somewhere,
going to England and went to England because he wanted to steal all the
*   money of all the banks,*
stole ten already, stole all the banks in New York,
and going to New South Wales and stole some more banks,
and after that no one's going to reckernise him because new clothes, dye hair,
wear a beard, and nobody reckernise him ever and won't steal any more
banks because going to be a millionaire,
and he's got a bruvver and his bruvver's just the same as him,
doesn't steal banks, but just as mad as him,
all his family is—I can't understand all that writing!—
his brother's trying to get him out of trouble and that,
they went to this party, and everybody said, "He's mad, he steals banks,"
and his brother said, "Let's go steal some banks,"
and he stole a lot of banks,
and was in that many fights he broke his arms, his legs, his ribs, his nose,
he broke his fingers from everyone bashing into him,
and then he got killed. That's all.

82. The King Who Was Peter

by Joey, seven, who has already burnt out a house and two cars, and seems always
fidgeting to touch and destroy things. Home life is very unsettled and "fathers"
and "uncles" change. In this story can be seen the anger which drives him to burn
and destroy.

    The boy's first drawing was at a three-year-old level—a face with streamers—but
he attempted a second, which did have a body, limbs and crown, like the King in
the story they had just had in class. Joey was eager and delighted to have attention
all to himself, but could not keep still even so. He continually interrupted his own
story to try to have a go at a projector and film unfortunately left on the table. However, his only breakage was accidental—the pencil lead.

There was a king
and he was Peter
and he saw this child
and he—a giant said to the man not to come near his home,
he's got—he's a monster,
and he's a bear,
and he turns into a bat,
and he scares people.
And he—the man pinches the man's money,
he goes to a shop and steals,
he goes to a golf club,
he smashes the window,
he steals some money,
he smashes someone's head off,
he smashes a car,
he smashes his crown,
he smashes his hat,
he smashes his pot, he smashes his cup, he smashes a plane, and he
* smashes a boat,*
he smashes it all up.
He smashes the projector,
like that.
He smashes a drum, he smashes a drum again, he smashes a gun.
He gets a ash-tray and smashes it on someone's head.
He's been smashing all these things.
(Does anyone like him?)
A bum, a dog, a bastard and a shit.
(Does he like anyone?)
He likes you.
(And what can he make?)
He can't make anything.

83. Eddie, the Evil Devil

by Angelo, nine. Stories of inner-urban boys on the way to becoming aggressive
delinquents often show that instead of having omnipotent ideas about success as
"baddies", they already have, at some level, an expectation of disaster and retribu-
tion. Their attitude in some ways resembles Milton's Lucifer, as in this story by a
nine-year-old migrant boy on the edge of a gang of older boys.

He's an evil devil, and he doesn't give any cats (chance)
He's going to give them one more chance.
He's got this book, and reads this book,
and sees you near,

and it puts an evil spell on you,
he's gonna turn out to be the worst devil,
and some angels'll come up and kill them,
and all the country,
all the world, will be in peace without him,
Eddie the Evil Devil.

84. No One Wins

by Carlos, eight, a Spanish boy whose outbursts of aggression seem related to his lonely mother's breakdown in acute depression. His second story, about a "person", was of a giant monster who ate people up, threw rocks on a ship, thought he was strong and went crashing houses and roofs, and was killed by another monster.

Two space ships attacking themselves,
another planet wants to destroy the world,
and the earth won,
and after he want destroy the earth,
and they both destroy themselves,
sort of like bombs and guns.

85. The End of It All

by Alan, ten, who was asked to dictate a story that he could then copy out in his work-book of Creative Writing to show his class-teacher. The first line of the story began formally enough, but then he forgot what the exercise was about, and became more and more involved in the story, as it became worse and worse.

This is how it can feel for a very small child—when one baby elephant is in trouble, it is a cosmic event. However, when older children—and adults—project their own suffering and revenge on to the screen of the whole world, there can be disastrous consequences.

A large elephant went out to play
and his friend elephants wouldn't let him play
and they bashed him up,
and he was crying, and his Mum told them off and said,
"Don't do it again."
And his Dad punched them all up
and so did his grandfather
and his grandnan
and his Mum
and hisself.
And then they said, "How do you like that?"

And they said they didn't like it.
And they punched them up again,

and they ran inside crying.
And their mothers came out and bashed everyone up,
and their grandfather and grandma and Mum and Dad,
even the poor little elephant got punched up.

And they got some more frends and punched them all up.
And everyone in the world punched everyone up,
and the world blew up,
and all the cars bashed up,
and all the houses blown up

and there was nothing left.

YOU NEVER LEARN

There is a common belief that people learn from their mistakes, and some even believe that it is necessary to let children make mistakes rather than teach them how to avoid them. This is only partly true, and true only for some situations. The lives of "disadvantaged" adults often show what "disadvantaged" children's stories show by intuition, that they will wreck their lives by making the same mistakes over and over again, as if they are on a wheel of fate and cannot get off.

86. The Little Girl and the Giant

by Kellie, ten. Kellie at ten illustrates "the girl who asked for trouble". The antecedents of the final rape/murder here are an unpopular, unlikeable child who found affection and attention through a first incident. Here the attention and the sympathy were awarded following an attack on her; in other cases the flattery of the man or the commotion caused can substitute, however unsatisfactorily, for the love she really desires.

Once upon a time a little girl was walking in the forest and a giant
  showed up and she—
she was scared, so she ran back home and told the woodcutter, and the
  woodcutter said, "Don't worry about him, he is my friend."
And she said, "I was scared the first time."
They used to call him the Hunchback.
They still do.
After that, he attacked the little girl, so had to get his head chopped off.
All the people were happy, and they liked the little girl a lot more,
cos they never used to like her, they used to tease her,
because she used to be naughty to her mother and say bad things,
and they never liked her or talked to her.

One day, she was walking again in the forest, and the sun was shining,
and she met this other—
she met a man, and the man said, "Hullo," and the little girl ran, and the
woodcutter came along and the little girl called, "Help! Help!"
The woodcutter said, "What is the matter?" and the little girl cried,
"There's a man in the forest, and he asked me how I was."
And the woodcutter came along with her, and chopped off his head.

And the little girl walked in the forest again, and met a man, and this time
the little girl was taken away, and her mother was petrified, because she
couldn't find her.
All of a sudden, the little girl escaped, and she lost her way in the forest.
And a man came along. He was the woodcutter, but she didn't know, and
she goes, "Help! Help!" And the woodcutter said, "What's the
matter?" and she said, "A man tried to kidnap me."

And the man came along, and he kidnapped her, and hit the woodcutter on
the head and cut his head off, and then the man told the little girl, "If
you don't be quiet, I'll kill you."
And the little girl was crying now because the man caught her. It was
getting late and she wanted to go home.

And she escaped again. And the man caught her. And then the man killed
her|

And then the police came along, and he was put in jail for a murder
charge, fined of 5000 dollars.
That's all.

87. The Bikie's End

by John, thirteen, who is truanting from school. He says he traunts because at school they are only "mucking around" in idealistic open programmes, but he stayed away from formal classes when he was younger as well. He has always been in trouble, and he—and his mother—always behave as if he has never been in trouble before: he is a "good boy", and it is unjust and unfair that he should be picked on by the authorities, when other boys are so much worse, when he is innocent, when he was pushed into it, and so forth.

In his stories, however, John is not a good boy. What he does is done deliberately, with open eyes. And it can be seen that he expects and even anticipates punishment and final execution by society, yet he will commit crime after crime until that happens.

At this stage, we cannot tell what originally happened to John and when, to set him on the path towards this hopeless delinquency. The home is disturbed, but John is now one of the disturbers in it.

He's a bikie, and he's just been arrested by the police for disturbing the
peace, and put in jail for two years.

And when he gets out
he does the same thing again
and it happens again.
And he tears down the police station and gets out again,
and they don't see him again./
Nothing happens. He goes to a hut out in the bush and he kills the bloke
   that lives in there, cos it's got all food and that in it,
and the police have been tracking him
and he gets caught and he gets hung.

88. The Repeater

by Sandro, six, the youngest child in a "family with problems", beset by social
workers for every member of the family and for a variety of disabilities and disorders.
The father is a periodical appearer, but there are also other male figures, some of
whom the children claim have interfered with them. Sandro spent much of his early
years inside a high-rise flat, sometimes alone. At school he is described as having the
"bee-in-a bottle-syndrome", unable to sit down and concentrate on anything for
more than a few seconds, and he is generally boisterous and oppositional. He can
sometimes be managed by asking him to do one thing in order to provoke him to
do the opposite. He tears up his work every day, particularly if his teacher admires
it or says it is good.

   Sandro's story shows how, even at six, children may have "learnt not to learn".
Even at six, they may have internalised the hate they feel the world has for them.
They hate themselves. It is because they care for nobody, not even themselves, that
later the world will feel the consequences of their hate as it spreads beyond them.

Jump out the window.
Gonna walk to the window, climb out the window
And jump off the roof.
Kill hisself.
Cos get into the hoppital,
then he'll get needle.
He'll come out of hoppital and do it again/
Kill hisself again.
Jump out of the window.

THE STORY OF ONE CHILD'S LIFE

The last story in this collection is also the longest. It was poured out by a little boy of seven who had just been put in an orphanage, and it was told with such matter-of-factness combined with urgency to tell it, that there is reason to see in it his symbolic autobiography. Stephen had already told a story about being in hospital and being visited by his Mum and Dad—an obvious translation of his present situation and of what the orphanage authorities possibly promised him—but when he was asked to tell "any story you like", the dam broke. The story went on for forty-five minutes without any pause except for an enforced stop with the bell at playtime. When the bell rang again, his mind was still burdened, for there he was sitting at the table again, and he went on with his story as if there had been no break at all. When he finally wound down, as if all the story had been told out of him, the restless characters in his story were put to sleep, and Stephen laid his own head down on the table.

This, perhaps more than any other story in this book, can take you into a world of childhood no adult author could ever describe.

You will also find in it themes and beginnings of themes which are further developed in the shorter stories of the other children.

89. When Am I Going?

by Stephen, seven.

About cats and lions, then they will roar,
and the King of the lions will see they was eaten,
and then the lion roars at the King, and the lion said, he said,
"I'm going away."

He put on the kettle, the King lion, and then they had a cup of tea
before they went hunting to kill people,
and then they went hunting, and then they killed men, six men,
and then they had some more people to eat and the King had a cup of tea
*　　again.*
And the King had his tea, and then he went hunting again, and then he got
*　　some football players and ate them, and then he catched some kangaroos*
*　　for the baby ones, the baby lions,*
and then he was happy, because he got 100 people,
and the next day he caught 60 people, and then he got fat,
and he couldn't go to sleep because he was going to have another baby,
and then he didn't eat any more food and he let the baby lions eat it,
because he couldn't get up because he was having another baby.

And when he had the baby, he got up, and then when the baby came
*　　out of his stomach, he said, "I'm happy, I've got another baby,*
Give this baby some food after one day,
We will catch some food for the baby, it is time,
and then the baby will be big like me."

The baby would be little, and when he gets the baby he's going to feed them
and when he gets up he said to the baby,
he's going to kill all the people in the world,
and he's going to eat them.
And then they ate them, and then the whole family got big like giants,
and they couldn't get the people because the people were too small,
and they had to poke their tongue out to kill the people.

And there were soldiers, and then the soldiers ran for it,
and then they said, "The lions are bigger than us, let's run through the
*   jungle."*
"I'll hide in this tree," one soldier said,
"I'll hide in this wheelbarrow," another soldier said,
and then another soldier said, "I'm going up in the tree with the other
*   soldier.*
We will get ready to jump on the tiger with our knifes.
You go on one tiger and I'll go on another."
And then they killed two lions, but the other two lions got away,
and then after the people win, the two baby lions come and got the knife out
*   of his Mum's back,*
and then his Mum wasn't alive but the other one come alive,
but his Mum was just dead a little bit,
and then they buried his Mum and then they stayed,
and then they made a fire near their Mum,
and then they made a candle out of wax.
And then his Mum woke up and said, "rrrrrh, rrrrh,"
and then they buried him up fast.

And then he said, "Let's go through the jungle and look up at the trees this
*   time."*
And he said, "Who are you? I don't know who are you,"
and then the baby lion said, "I'm Frank," and "I'm Tom,"
and then they said, he said, "Look, what's my name?
I don't know what's my name."
And then he said, "My name is ... . Tom."
And then they said there was two Toms, and then they ran through the
*   jungle.*
And then the baby one said, "Stop! I got a sore leg,"
and then they stopped.
And then they said, "I'm going, I don't care about you," and they said that
*   you're lazy.*
and they said, "Let's get up, I'm not lazy."
And then they said, "Let's go, I don't want to stay here this long,

It's too smelly here. It smells like the beach.
I got a good idea, Let's go to the beach.
There will be people here so we can eat them."
But the mother said, "No, don't go, you might eat the sand instead of the
*   people,*
and if you eat the sand, then you will die."
And then the lion will be fat, and then before the baby didn't come out,
and then he had three babies.
And then he said don't go to the beach any more because you can drown.
"Next time when we go to the beach, we will take our lifesavers,
and I'll swim out to sea and you babies stay here,
and if you don't stay, I won't catch any fish."
And they said to the King, "It's too busy,"
and then he said, "I'll catch some eels too and crabs."
And then he went further and further under the car bridge,
and a car came over and fell on top of the lion,
and then the lion died and then the babies lived,
and then the lion, the baby lions said, "He's died two times,
*   We can't save him now.*
*   How come we don't die?"*
"Because we been just born, and we need to be old to die."
And then he said, "Let's go, before we go, we'll get
*   some milk and some water and fish and crabs*
and eels.
But before we go, we gotta pray.
And then we'll go and then we'll run away,
and then we won't worry."

And then they said, "Let's go, it's too busy."
And then they said, "Let's go or I'll bash you up,
Because if you don't come, I'll stab you,
And then if you don't come, I'll eat you.
Before we go, I'm going to eat your mother."
"You can't do that!"
"Are you going to stop me? If you stop me I'll kill you.
If you dob me, I'll kill you with a knife, you won't have no head left.
Are you coming? Or else I'll run away from you."
"I'm running now, see ya."
"I'm going to get some army to kill you and shoot you so you can die
because you're not my friend."
"Why aren't you my friend? Tell me, why aren't you my friend?
If you're not my friend, I'm going to run away."

"*And if you run away, I won't be a friend for ever and ever.*"
"*All right, I'll stay with you, so you won't get hurt.*"
"*And then if you run away, I won't be a friend for years and years and*
years."
"*I don't care, I'm going to run away now.*"
And then he said, "When are we going?"
And he said, "Wait until my mother gets alive.
Before we die, we got to save her to help us,
and then when we save her, she will be . . .
she won't growl any more,
she will be happy,
and then she'll say,
'*I'm happy, because how did you save me?*' "
And then the baby lion said, "We just got you on our backs,
and then we buried a hole, and then we put you in a hole so you won't die."
And then they were happy.
And then they said, "I'm going away."
"*Where are you going?*"
"*I'm going to the beach.*"
"*No, don't go to the beach. You know before you ate 10,000 people, and if*
you eat any more, you will be sick."
"*No I won't, I'm not fat any more. I am skinny. Why am I skinny?*
I shouldn't be skinny, I should be fat."

And then they went to the gardens, they had fish'n chips and a cup of coffee
and one big chocolate drink and then ten people.
And then they said, "Yummy."
Then they said, "Let's have some bubblegum, bubblegum's nice,
but if it gets stuck in our teeth, we'll have no teeth left."
Then the lion said, "Wanna make a bet?"
And he said, "Orright, I'll make a bet. Ten thousand dollars."
And then it did get stuck in the mother's teeth,
and then they said, "Now I owe you ten thousand dollars. Why did you
run away?"
"*Because it's no good here,*
and you can go over that side and I'll go over that side and then you go on
that side."
And then the lion said,
"*Oh, let's go to bed, it's midnight now, we've been up so late.*"
"*You go to bed, I'll stay in day.*
If there's any people here, I'll keep them for breakfast."
"*What about lunch?*" "*I'll get you a thousand.*"

Then he said, "I don't want a thousand for lunch, I want ten for lunch, get
me 30, we'll have ten each, and if we have ten, we'll be fulled up after
all of them,
after we finish we'll be sick,
and then when we are sick, you will vomit.
But if you be sick, you'll have to go to hospital."
Then he said, "If I go to hospital because of you, I'm going to bash you
up."
Then the baby said, "I thought you gonna be happy."
And then he said, "Oh yeah, I forgot that.
Let's go and get lots of lions and cents
and then we'll be happy."
"But why we be happy?" I said.
"I don't know why we're going to be happy."

And then the lion said, "Let's go and get a whole jungle, and then he'll get
a whole lot, and then we'll have thousands.
Then we'll be good. Then we'll have lots of good times."
And then we went, then the babies said, "Let's go to ..."
And then they went to go, and then they said, "Let's go now, we can't wait.
It will be good if we go now."
And then they went got 1000s and 100s and then they said, "Let's go.
Now will be a good time. And then we'll play a game."
And then they played hopscotch.
And after hopscotch they played spinning tops. And then they went through
the jungle.
There was a lake. And they swam in it.
And when it was midnight, they went to bed and then they went fast asleep
after they dried theirself,
and then they went for another swim back to their place that their ...

And the King bought a house.
And then after they bought a house, they slept in it and slept in it and
they don't go away from the house they stayed in the house,
Because they were scared.
And after that they went through the lake, and then they found another
house.
And then they had two houses. They didn't know what to do with the
houses.
The second house was no good. The first house was good.
And then they chopped down the second house,
Because it is no good. And they had to have a fire near their house,
and then they burnt the tree down, chucked five trees on the fire.

and then the fire went out and after the fire they went to the lake to catch
  some fish.

The King said, "I'm not going in the water, but let's get some fishing
  rods."
The baby said, "Let's go at midnight to the lake."
"No, it will be too cold." And after that they said,
"When are we going back home?" And after that they said,
"When are we going? When are we going?" And after that they said,
"I wanna go home." So they said, "I'm going home now."
And then they said, "I'm going home now. See ya." And then they said . . .
then they prayed.
And after they pray, they went to sleep on the grass with blanket over them,
and then after that morning, in the afternoon a car came and nearly went
  over them,
and the car driver hopped out and said, "Are you lions all right?"
And then he said, "Lions!" and then he ran away.
And after that he said, "I'm going. I don't like this place."
So the driver went off in his car and he shot bullets at the lions.
And then they said, "When are we going? This is too busy."
And they said,
"I wanna go straight away now." And then they said,
"I'm going now. I'm going. It's too dark. It is past midnight."
And then they went to bed the next morning

And the next morning they thought and thought what to do and then they
  said,
"We've got to pray."
They just prayed.
And after that they went away in the jungle.
And then they said, "When are we going?"
And after that we got some oranges in the jungle, and when we got some
  oranges we'll get a whole basketful.
And after that, they ate oranges. And then they said,
"When are we going? I wanna go."
And this one baby one was nine years old, and then the other baby one was
  six years old and then the mother was thirteen years old, and the father
  was—eighty years old.
And there was nobody else. There was only four in the family,
and but they had another baby, and that baby was one years old and one
  day,
and then they had no more babies.
and after no more babies, they went to bed, and next morning they got

oranges and oranges,
a whole carful.
And then they went in their car to the lake, and then they stopped on the
road,
and then they nearly tipped over, this car knocked them over in the middle of
the road,
and after he did get knocked over in the road they were sad, not happy.

And after they weren't happy, they seen a frog, and the lion jumped in and
got it,
and then they ate it, they said it was a giant one that leaved the eggs in a
bottle
and then one egg hatched and then they had a frog,
and when that frog gone big, they got the eggs out of it,
and then they ate the frog and after the frog was born, they got more eggs
out of the frog,
and then they keeped on.
And they said, "When are we going? It is too late. Let's go now.
It is too busy. I'm going now."
It is not too busy. It is early, not midnight.
And when it was daytime, it won't be dark and dark.
And at midnight, creatures came out, and cats,
and after the cats, a big lion came out and said, "Can I be in your group?"
And then there was five, and then he said, "I'll pay for a room.
That is, if you give me one. Can you give me four rooms for my family?"
And when he got four rooms, he let two in one room and two in another
room, and then another one in another room, and they went to sleep.
And after they went to sleep, they said, "We forgot to pray, let's pray in
bed." They just prayed.
And when they finished breakfast, they prayed.
At every mealtime they pray.
And then they said, "I want to go now, Let's go," and after they went,
they said,
"I will go now." And after they went, they said,
"I'm going."
And then they stopped near a little forest and sleeped there in bed.
There was four beds, and then one had to sleep on the ground, where it was
muddy.
And the one that sleeped on the ground got his pillow dirty and his mattress
dirty and his blanket dirty.
And at midnight creatures came out and a car came, and a creature jumped
on top of the car, and the car ran, and then the car shot the creature,

and then after the creature got shot, the creature fell off,
and after the creature fell off, the creature was dead and it came back to normal.
And after it came back to normal, it came alive,
and after it came alive, it chased the car.

The car was going slowly; the car wasted petrol. One man had to put his petrol in the back of the car and the car stopped and the lion was walking, so he hopped out of his car and put petrol in and then ran away in the forest and the lion was near him and he ran in the car and ran right away,
and then the creature came and tried to kill him,
and after the creature came, he jumped on the front of the car and laid down so he can't see where he's going,
and after when he didn't see where he can go he went to bed.
And he laid in his car and he had a smash.
And he forgot to turn his car on and forgot to lock the doors,
and the creature came in and got him and clapped him and he woke up,
and then after he woke up, the creature drove the car and ran the man over.

And the man was dead and the creature ran away and a man was chasing him so the creature turned around and ran the man over,
and the creature said that there was 1000s of enemy, there was 1000s of them.
And then the lion and the creature ran in the car, there was no more petrol,
because there was lots of people and the gorilla hopped out of the car,
and they came on and hit the gorilla on the head and then the gorilla fell down
and then the Lion's family hopped in and then they killed another lion,
and chucked him out,
and the car went to the petrol station to get half a gallon of petrol,
and then after they got their petrol they ran away and then they didn't come back, they only went back to their house,
and after they went to their house it was midnight so they went to bed
and after they went to bed they prayed.
Then they said, "I should get to sleep" and then the other Lion said, "I think you should go to sleep now."

And then the Baby Lion went to sleep fast as a creature,
because he was awake until midnight,
and after midnight he was asleep in one minute and he didn't wake up in the morning.
His Dad had to get the belt to wake him up.

And he said, Dad, he didn't want his breakfast,
so his Dad said, "All right, don't have your breakfast, I'll have your
breakfast,"
and after his Dad had the breakfast he was fat as a dog.
And then he ran right away to get some milk and then he drank the milk
right up he had to ran away to get some more milk.
When he went to bed he climbed out of the window.
And after he went out the window his Dad—his Dad went into his bed and
he jumped out the window and his Dad got a shotgun and went after him,
and he ran right into the forest and his Dad went after him,
and after his Dad went hunting, his Dad couldn't find him, but when his
Dad went to go through the forest he was hiding from him behind a tree,
and then he climbed up in a tree and then he sat up on top of the tree,
and then he climbed up in a tree and he sat up on top of the tree,
and when his Dad came past he dropped rocks on his head,
and his Dad said, "It is raining," and then he ran back to the house to get
his raincoat and then he forgot to put his helmet,
so the little Baby Lion put his helmet on and then he jumped on top of him
and then he chucked helmets on top of him
and then he said, "Helmet rain's coming down."
And then he said, "I'm going to get a helmet, it's raining, I forgot my
helmet."
And then he went to put his helmet on and then it melted because it was only
frozen like a Sunny-Boy.
And the sun came out and he put a helmet on and then it melted,
every time he put a helmet on it melted
and he put a plastic helmet on and then it—the sun burnt it,
and then he made some glass and then he sleep in it,
and then the sun was hot in the night time and so the grass blew up,
and after the grass blew up, he was still asleep,
and then he woke up and then he was black,
like a black cat
and then he said, "I look like a black cat."
And then the family woke up and said, "Look, there's a black cat, let's
kill it."
And he said, "I belong to your family, I got burnt from grass."
And then they shot arrows at him and then they said, "Stop, that's our Dad.
I'm running away from here, let's drop stones on his head."
And then they got a big rock, and after they got a big rock they chucked it on
his head, and after they got a rock they said,
"Let's drop it on his head again, his helmet will break into little stones."

And after his helmet broke, he went away, and after he went away, he went
  through the forest,
and after he went through the forest, he ran right away
that no one can see him.
And then he found his skin in the grass
and he sticked it with glue on himself
and then he went away and they shot arrows at him,
and then they said, "Hey that's our Dad," and they went to sleep,
and after they went to sleep, they said, they said, "Let's go to bed,"
and after they went to sleep they said, "Let's go to bed,"
and after they went to bed, they said, "Let's go to bed!"
. . . and then . . .
and after they went to bed . . .
I don't know any more . . . .

Eight months later, Grade II had to write a composition on anything they liked.
Most of the children copied about half a page from each other on "I went for a walk
and I saw . . ." and similar subjects. This little boy took quite a while writing his
essay which said simply, "I am cowing hoem."

Some of this story derives quite directly from the little boy's present experiences;
he is clearly quite impressed by all the praying that goes on in the orphanage, for
example, and some of the uneasy relationships among the boys also comes through.

The constant "When am I going?" is not only an undercurrent among all the
orphanage children who retain any hope, but is also, in its various manifestations in
the story, an expression of the insecurity and driven need to escape with nowhere to
escape to, that characterise so many unstable families and their buffeted children.
It is one among the distinct genre of stories told by boys aged five to twelve that could
be called "The Running Boys" (see p. 97). The little boys themselves may be delinquents, or "hyperactive", or suffering from "behaviour disorders", maltreated,
rejected or neglected.

The stories characteristically tell of boys still roaming the streets at midnight, of
families continually on the move, of running to escape from haunted settings, or
being lost and never found, of helpless, pathetic and even malignant parents, of
children on whom falls the burden of organising survival, and a society and environment that are hostile and dangerous.

The world is a confused and chaotic place, and things happen as meaninglessly
as in television watched as the children watch it, casually, without wondering about
beginnings or waiting for the end.

In this story we see children's astonishing capacity for symbolism (yet some people
think that the concreteness of children's thinking means they cannot understand
anything beyond "John and Betty" stories!). Here we have a child's experience of
family life—an insecure family in a world agin it, with the typical tragic mother-
figure whom the children try to protect, the ambiguous, ambivalent and sometimes
hateful father-figure, the child's own confusion about who and what and why he is,
his attempts to make meaning out of life, the unpredictability of events and of adult
decisions, and the fears and the anxieties, so that the instinctive attitude to any
stranger is "Shoot it".

To me, this story is like Shakespeare—it is full of quotations, which say in a few words more about a child's experiences than could pages of careful description.

Then the baby said, "I thought you gonna be happy."
And then he said, "O yeah, I forgot that.
Let's go and get lots of lions and cents
and then we'll be happy."
"But why we be happy?" I said.
"I don't know why we're going to be happy."

For children of seven, questions of life and death and love and hate can be very real—but they are left alone to puzzle them out.

. . . the baby lions said, "He's died two times,
We can't save him now.
How come we don't die?"
"Because we been just born and we need to be old to die."
And then he said, "Let's go, before we go, we'll get some milk and some
water and fish and crabs
and eels.
But before we go, we gotta pray.
And then we'll go and then we'll run away,
and then we won't worry. . . ."

And then they said, "Let's go, or I'll bash you up,
Because if you don't come, I'll stab you,
And then if you don't come, I'll eat you.
Before we go, I'm going to eat your mother."
"You can't do that!"
"Are you going to stop me? If you stop me I'll kill you,
If you dob me, I'll kill you with a knife, you won't have no head left. . . ."

And then they shot arrows at him and then they said, "Stop, that's our Dad.
I'm running away from here, let's drop stones on his head."
And then they got a big rock, and after they got a big rock they chucked it on
his head . . .

And his Mum was dead, but "his Mum was dead just a little bit".

The stories—and actions—of older boys show what is only too likely to happen to this very sensitive, honest, open little boy. When the baby lions grow up, they "go hunting to kill people".

The Prevention of Violence

It must surely be reckoned one of the glories of our time, that in an age which has seen so much destruction, the nation's care for its children has reached a degree unknown before in history. Research and learning have gone together to discover the basic needs for the healthy development of the child from before his birth to the end of school life . . .

Phyllis Hostler, *The Child's World.*

Many of these stories reveal that children come to believe that there is "no way" before they have even been given a chance to find any. Adults echo this catch-cry, "What's the use?" without allowing themselves a chance to try to solve the children's problems.

The age-old problem of the disinherited in all societies may never completely disappear, no matter how it may change, but it is always a challenge.

Children are always the final victims of social injustice, and reforms are needed in the aims of employment policies, immigration, housing, the economic bases for child-rearing, and facilities for home life. Different times and places require different types of reforms, and any reforming policy must take into account the necessity to counter the swing of the pendulum as it veers from one extreme attitude to another.

PSYCHOLOGICAL POVERTY

"Social disadvantage" is a term bedevilled by assumptions that "middle class" necessarily means "advantage" and "working class" is the same as deprivation. But this is of course not the case. "Social disadvantage" means the existence of social conditions that few disagree should be changed, and of psychological conditions that can cause childhood problems regardless of social class and subculture.

From a psychologist's point of view, a "disadvantaged" child may come from any socio-economic group. He is a child deprived of the right to grow in faith or hope or love, because adults have betrayed, damned or rejected him, and he can only use destruction to make his mark on the world. Aggression can be a substitute when a child is denied competence.

It is not a matter of social class when parents do not know how to love or how to manage a handicapped or difficult child; when they take for granted the right to yell at, or belt their children as if they themselves were still uncontrolled children; when they scramble up their adult relationships or reduce their own humanity with drugs or alcohol regardless of the emotional needs of the children who are captive watchers. And it is not a matter of class when adults acquire children as if they were acquiring television sets to be switched on or off, and are surprised and shocked to find that young, live human beings are not as "instantly" rewarding or disposable as the usual run of consumer goods.

Children may be battered, merely bashed, or just picked up and put down when irresponsible adults feel like it. But the children still learn not to learn—because what you learn only hurts—and not to love—because the young roots of love are only pulled up. They also learn that they must be rotten bad to be so unloved—and the only thing children can do with this knowledge is to *be* bad. In their stories, all these developments can be seen.

Many aspects of our culture combine to transmit a dislike and disregard for children. As always happens, it is those at the bottom of the social scale who most show the effects of the social pathology of the whole. Organic theories of society are not merely poetical in suggesting that every part and aspect affects every other—they all tend to jerk together. When one part seems diseased, look at the whole body, and do not try to cure only by local application.

The industrial suburbs are like a prism, focusing the stresses and unfair demands that our society puts on all its children through its realities, its fantasies, its destruction, aggression and conspicuous waste. And this is in addition to all the problems that must be faced anywhere, any time, in being a child and in growing up.

Practical measures to reduce the inheritance of "psychological poverty" must include the recognition that to have a child is a privilege—not a right or a duty or a burden imposed by outside forces. Social pressures could change emphasis, to prevent rather than encourage begetting and conception without readiness to love and care for the incredible "body products" of sex. The State must realise what poor quality machine-fodder is produced when reproduction is desired only for feeding economic or military machines.

There cannot be rules about ideal child-rearing to apply to every child, but we do know a great deal about what should be avoided, and about how to enjoy children. Practical community education can begin in childhood itself, with real "practice" through closer links between schools, homes and community. Children should learn the Facts of Living, not just the Facts of Life.

CHILDREN WHO SURVIVE

No matter how awful the environment and how adverse the circumstances, some children seem able to survive apparently undamaged, like a flower in dustbin alley. The existence of such children is sometimes used as evidence that things as they are do not need to be changed—if they can grow up to become normal law-abiding citizens, why can't the others? And so we continue to try to change the children, and not the problems that produced them.

It would take a second book to show from the children's own stories how they do survive, and what distinguishes them from the children who fail, and hate, and hit back.

But since it is easy to lose perspective when every story in a book (or everything in your environment) treats themes in a similar way, reflecting the same underlying attitudes, three stories by "ordinary" happy children are included here.

The subjects are similar. Two are about plane crashes, by middle-class children doing well at school, and from happy homes. Contrast them with Stories 49 (p. 85), 50 (p. 85), 81 (p. 124), and 84 (p. 128). Significant features are the "realism" of detail and cause and effect, the logic of sequences and consequences, the lively interest in the whole environment, but above all, the competence and optimism of the heroes. These children tend to see the solutions to difficulties and crises to lie in the heroes themselves, who can use their initiative, courage and skill to escape from their predicaments.

The third story is by the son of a prosperous business family living in the inner suburbs. Like the stories of so many inner-urban children, it is tragic. The hero is overwhelmed by the odds against him and is killed. The contrast, however, is in the sense of purpose and heroism, and of a sacrifice that was not in vain and brings immortality with it. Like the other two stories, it does not end at a crisis point unsolved, as do so many other narratives in this book which are only concluded for a curious listener by the prompting, "and what happened then?" There is form, and a conclusion. The narrator as well as the hero is, in the end, the controller of events.

Two Aeroplane Crashes

to contrast with Stories 49 (p. 85), 50 (p. 85), 81 (p. 124) and 84 (p. 128).

Flying High

by Neil, ten.

> *Shall it be a detailed picture or what? (No, that would take a long time.)*
> *Well, it takes off from the airfield in the distance,*
> *and I took off in my Tiger Moth round here, and flew for about two miles to the south,*
> *and I was away up about 200 feet altitude, 2000 feet, 200 feet,*
> *and I heard a splutter and my engine conked out and I suddenly realised I had engine trouble!*

*Anyway the engine just stopped dead completely, I couldn't make it work
    again,*
and I started diving down, and then put myself into a shallow glide,
and managed to land in a nearby paddock,
*and it was found out later that a fuel pipe had been completely clogged up.
Full stop.*

The Heroic Pilot

by George, nine.

This plane flew from Sydney to Perth.
*Left Sydney at 4 a.m. and has just flown over Alice Springs when a storm
    came up and there is a thunderstorm and there was a great downpour of
    rain, and lots of flashes of lightning.*
And then a terrible thing happened
a- some lightning struck the tail of the plane
and it started breaking and it set fire to the plane
and the pilot turned round and headed back to Alice Springs.
He had to make a crash landing at Alice Springs,
and fire engines and ambulances came there
and it came down and crashed into the runway
and the ambulances and fire-brigades came over to try to put the fire out,
and rescue the people.
There was 96 there was 96 people aboard and they climbed out of the back,
because the firemen chopped the tail off so then they could escape that way.
*The pilot was trapped because a wall of fire was burning the cabin wall,
    burning it down,*
*so he smashed the cockpit window and threw the glass at the fire that he has
    smashed and then he jumped out.*
*There was a few people had broken their legs and one person had broken
    his arm,*
The pilot had got quite a few cuts from jumping through the broken glass.
The whole plane was destroyed except for the radio which the pilot used,
he pulled it from the control board so it wouldn't blow up.

*And then in a few days they sent for another plane to fly from Sydney to
    Alice Springs so the passengers could fly on, and they made it safely
    there again.*

A Tragic War Story

He Died With His Own Will

by Andrew, ten. This is almost the only war-story in the collection by inner-city children in which there is a hero with any individuality or purpose, and a concept of courage which is explicitly recognised. The bright boy who told the story was the widely-travelled son of a well-off family.

This plane is going along in the second world war, it's a
Hurricane, it's British, and the war is against Germany,
1939 or 1940 this war was.
The Germans were fighting, the Germans beat the French people,
and then this Hurricane had to go up and try to shoot down
nineteen Messerschmitts,
and got down then and then had one behind and one in front and
didn't know what to do so goes up out of it,
and the one behind it came right down and the Hurricane dived
and came back up again and got them both and got twelve.
It got shot in the back tail but it was all right and just
got up again, and then as it was going down again shot three
more and fifteen were left,
and swooping down to get him he got shot,
and as he was shooting Messerschmitts he died himself,
and so on his grave they put a memorable thing,
they put the verse on his grave,
He Died With His Own Will.
He was very brave and he tried his hardest to get all the
Messerschmitts down but unfortunately he died shooting down
the last one.

CHILDREN WHO ARE VULNERABLE

Unlike the three "survivors" quoted above, most of the children in this book were unhappy and disturbed in their behaviour, and obsessional and limited in their imaginations, so that only glimpses appeared of their other potentialities. They were developing destructive rather than constructive capacities and failing to learn how to love and how to maintain love.

Yet a remarkably high proportion of famous people have had early lives like theirs—bereaved, deprived, and even intolerable. These people were shaped and strengthened by the toughening experiences of their childhoods that may have distorted and weakened other, less able, personalities. However, this is not only a ruthless but a socially undesirable form of natural selection for greatness, since most of those who suffer too much too young are handicapped rather than made fitter. It does not benefit the species, because those who are damaged and should theoretically be "selected out", instead survive and multiply their kind.

There may conceivably be a genetic or constitutional component in much behaviour disorder, although it is cruelly mistaken to assume something is wrong in the family, physically or psychologically, for every child who is a little monster. Any child from any home can be touched by physical or neurological disorders, and the way his family rears him may perhaps only serve to reduce or exacerbate his chances of being a social liability. The concept of a "genetic pool" in the community can include the value of having as wide a variety of capacities and potentials in a society as possible, and making the most of them in every way. The child who shows "sociopathic" or other "deviant" tendencies might not be doomed to become an anti-social or asocial adult if his apparent handicaps could be developed as assets, rather than hopeless attempts being made to change his whole personality into whatever particular model is held of the healthy person.

This means looking carefully at the way a culture gives children the language and "spectacles" by which they learn to identify, interpret and symbolise their experiences, and to direct their actions by socially-learnt expectations and attitudes. Children's early experiences form the basis of the idea of the world which they build up in their minds, which changes with new experiences but is never completely changed even if turned inside out. What children are able to learn later must fit that Procrustean bed already set up in their minds, however distorted that learning may then have to be.

That is why other people perceive a world unlike the world we see ourselves, and why individual children react differently to similar situations, as these stories show. An illustration is the way in which, in the same environment, boys' fantasies can explode with anger and violence, while girls', whether through conditioning or through biology, constrict into trivia and incorporate the attitudes of the victim.

Childhood lays down the range of ideas that are going to be open to us, the range of feelings that we can comprehend, the range of habits and behaviour patterns. The "given" of the temperament and physiology with which we are born interacts with the social climate around us, to set our levels of adaptation to pain, cruelty, noise, stimulation, and the other people in the world.

If this is so, we must look more carefully at what is done to "keep them quiet" during children's early years, because what is given to them then may be what they are given to later.

We must look more critically at what our society teaches children in the first seven years at home and school, and make it less destructive. Everyone, child and adult, needs more opportunities for creativity that is not disguised consumption, and more reliance on initiative to solve problems. No one should be set to making things that are "instant rubbish" in schools and factories, or to observing living people turned violently to instant rubbish, as entertainment.

Communal levels of stress and artificially-sustained excitement can be scaled down by deliberate attempts made by whoever can, wherever they can, so that things which are small and slow and peaceful and gentle and inexpensive can be enjoyed and appreciated as much as whatever is fast, big, explosive, violent and expensive.

We tend to take for granted the values and assumptions and directions of our culture. We may look again more carefully when we see them made explicit in the stories children tell.

SENTIMENTALITY AND REALISM

This book has been written with some feeling. It is not objective and scholarly, although it is based on an objective and scholarly study in progress. It may be labelled "sentimental", however, only insofar as there is any artificiality or falseness in the feeling, since that is what sentimentality means.

Sentimentality is basically callous. It is always a risk, but today, in order to avoid artificial "soft" feelings, hard and openly callous ones are exaggerated instead. "Exaggerated realism" is a form of sentimentality too.

And what can be more sentimental than to enjoy emotion of any sort, whether pathos, amusement, thrill or horror, that is evoked by others' suffering—and then do nothing!

The threads of this book are left in the hands of the reader, and they are mostly questions. Realism must include involvement. It is no help to these children just to let them tell stories.

Appendix I:

The stories presented in this book have been selected from two thousand. To show that the evidence is not merely anecdotal, some brief notes on a study of matched stories are included, illustrating the children's perceptions of four major aspects of life: the basic needs for food (and its symbolic equivalents), security, competence and relationships, together with an examination of fantasy and realism in the stories, and the effects of socio-economic class on sex differences.

The 170 stories analysed here were told by children eight to nine years old from eight "disadvantaged"* inner-urban Melbourne schools and five middle-class suburban schools, including two private schools. Fifty children in the disadvantaged schools were seen by their teachers to be particularly deprived, coming from disturbed homes lacking in love and care. All the other 120 children were "average", seen by their teachers to be neither bright nor dull, and without apparent problems.

THE EXPRESSION OF BASIC NEEDS
1. Food

Negative aspects—hunger, deprivation, poisoning, being devoured.
Positive aspects—nourishment, satisfaction, pleasure.

TABLE 1

FOOD AND DRINK IN STORIES TOLD BY CHILDREN
AGED 8–9 YEARS

Percentage incidence**

	N	Positive reference	Negative reference	None
Boys				
Suburban	30	27	3	70
Inner-urban	30	37	3	60
"Disadvantaged"	30	10	3	87
Girls				
Private school	20	30	10	60
Suburban	20	45	10	45
Inner-urban	20	40	15	45
"Disadvantaged"	20	20	10	70

Food and drink are common themes of younger children's stories, and children aged eight to nine still show considerable interest, although fewer make it their central theme. Girls are particularly concerned with orality, with references to meals and accounts of parties—or of poisoning, devouring, or being devoured.

Emotionally deprived children may tell stories of marvellous parties or of starvation, but at this age they often omit even incidental reference to food, which is possibly replaced in symbolic meaning by frequent themes of gaining riches and stealing. Also see Stories 1, 4, 5, 7, 19, 68, 77 and 87.

2. The Need for Security

Positive aspects—justified confidence of characters that reliable help and comfort available when needed

Anxiety as a normal experience—stories enlivened by dangers and crises but optimism about the outcome and readiness to use initiative to overcome

Negative aspects—catastrophe, unrelieved fears, inability to prevent disaster

all sources of help are unreliable or fail

* Socio-economic classification by the Australian Schools Commission.
** Statistical tests have not been considered appropriate; the subjective categories cannot always be defined precisely, and the findings of this small sample simply illustrate the features of the whole collection.

TABLE 2
ENVIRONMENTAL SECURITY IN STORIES TOLD BY
CHILDREN AGED 8–9 YEARS
Percentage incidence

	N	Security	Danger feared	Real danger
Boys				
Suburban	30	43	3	53
Inner-urban	30	27	9	63
"Disadvantaged"	30	7	3	90
Girls				
Private schools	20	40	10	50
Suburban	20	70	10	20
Inner-urban	20	55	30	15
"Disadvantaged"	20	20	–	80

TABLE 3
DEATH AND DAMAGE IN STORIES TOLD BY CHILDREN
AGED 8–9 YEARS
Percentage incidence

	Sub-urban girls N 40	Inner-urban girls N 20	Sub-urban boys N 30	Inner-urban boys N 30
No harm, physical or emotional	48	25	33	33
Physical punishment or ego hurt but no injury or death	15	45	3	7
Physical harm or conflict but death not stated explicitly	13	10	47	20
Annihilation explicitly stated	25	20	17	40
Death of central character	2	20	13	40

Anyone observing eight- to nine-year-old children can see how they often enjoy danger and fighting, particularly in fantasy. However, the greater insecurity shown in inner-urban children's stories does parallel the degree of insecurity in real life, and the frequency of death and punishment in their stories may be related to the fact that more often they see adults failing and suffering, and more often are the victims of circumstances themselves.

A fifth of the suburban girls and half the suburban boys describe a dangerous world, less than the inner-urban children, but the dangers appear greatest for the disadvantaged youngsters. Only 10 per cent of their stories are set in environmental security.

Although suburban boys' stories are often violent, injury is more likely than death, which is a common outcome in the inner-urban boys' narratives. Girls appear less adventurous and their central characters tend to be more passive and helpless (except in stories by the private-school girls). A greater need for security appears in their preference for settings and plots which involve no risk for the central characters, who rarely suffer in the suburban girls' stories, whatever happens to anybody else. The inner-urban girls are more likely to focus on hurt feelings or punishments for misdemeanours.

(All the stories in this book can be examined from these aspects.)

3. The Need for Competence

Positive aspects—showing initiative and achieving success through
  competence
Negative aspects—inability to help oneself or even try

TABLE 4
COMPETENCE OF CENTRAL CHARACTERS IN STORIES
TOLD BY CHILDREN AGED 8–9 YEARS
Percentage incidence

	N	**Passivity**	**Success**	**Failure**
Boys				
Suburban	30	24	43	33
Inner-urban	30	20	57	23
"Disadvantaged"	30	27	13	60
Girls				
Private schools	20	40	50	10
Suburban	20	50	20	30
Inner-urban	20	60	10	30
"Disadvantaged"	20	40	10	50

This analysis requires more elaboration than is possible here,
particularly for its connection with frustration and destructive behaviour as responses to expected failure.

Although girls from the élite independent schools tend to have
characters who succeed through their own or others' efforts, passivity
is generally marked in girls' stories.

The "disadvantaged" children are the most likely to tell stories
of complete helplessness and failure. In this sample only two of the
20 girls told a story with a successful outcome, and the boys' central
characters had a 60 per cent failure rate.

If story heroes try to do anything in girls' stories, the failure rate
rises from 10 to 30 to 50 per cent according to whether the narrators
attended independent schools, were "average" children at other
schools, or were "disadvantaged".

Also see stories such as 1, 5, 11, 12, 23, 24, 25, 27, 31, 37, 38, 47,
50, 52, 54, 73, 74 and 82.

4. The Need for Relationships

Positive aspects—emphasis on friendships and good relationships
Negative aspects—more significant enmities, or no relationships
  either friendly or hostile

TABLE 5
RELATIONSHIPS IN STORIES TOLD BY CHILDREN
AGED 8–9 YEARS
Percentage incidence

	N	Emphasis on good relation-ships	No relationships	Emphasis on hostile relationships
Boys				
Suburban	30	60	3	30
Inner-urban	30	40	–	60
"Disadvantaged"	30	27	10	63
Girls				
Private school	20	50	20	30
Suburban	20	60	10	30
Inner-urban	20	45	5	50
"Disadvantaged"	20	30	30	40

The more fortunate a child's social circumstances, the more likely
are his stories to emphasise comradeship, even in war stories, whereas
for disadvantaged children, especially the boys, personal encounter
is more likely to be marked by hostility.

THE THEMES AND SETTINGS
OF THE STORIES

TABLE 6

FANTASY AND REALISM IN STORIES TOLD BY
CHILDREN AGED 8–9 YEARS Percentage incidence

	N	Fantasy theme		Realistic theme	
		Familiar setting	Unfamiliar setting	Familiar setting	Unfamiliar setting
Boys					
Suburban	30	37	17	23	23
Inner-urban	30	13	47	20	20
Girls					
Suburban	40	40	10	50	–
Inner-urban	20	40	30	30	–

Girls show a preference for confining themselves to familiar settings, in contrast to inner-urban boys; middle-class children are more likely to be realistic in their narratives, however imaginative. Working-class boys of this age shun domestic settings, preferring streets, machines and space, but suburban boys will set their stories anywhere. Also see stories such as 1, 5, 6, 7, 9, 22, 26–34, 46, 48, 57, 61, 63, 66 and 86.

SEX AND SOCIAL CLASS DIFFERENCES

TABLE 7

SOME SEX DIFFERENCES IN STORIES BY GIRLS AND
BOYS AGED 8–9 YEARS

	Boys *N* 90 %	Girls *N* 80 %
Hero of same sex	72	56
Hero adult	47	9
Story involves vehicles	52	7
Story involves animals	21	54
Median *N* adjectives per story	2.5	7
Stories without adjectives	21	
Commonest adjective	big (23)	little (36)

Characteristics of boys' stories

In over a third there are aims of achievement, adventure, action, violence, and injury or death for the hero. Boys' stories are more often given a setting in place and time, which is also more often set outside the child's own personal experience, and both stories and drawings are usually given more realistic detail.

Characteristics of girls' stories

These tend to have familiar domestic settings or to be vague about place and time. They are more often like school readers or the whimsical and anthropomorphic stories adults often write for young children. The favourite adjective is "little", often in the context "little girl", while working-class boys prefer "big" and suburban boys prefer "fast", and few if any nine-year-old boys ever talk about "little boys".

Girls are more likely to express emotions, values and personal relationships in their stories, their peaceful and co-operative themes often appear more civilised, and overall their vocabulary is wider in range, particularly for adjectives.

It is possible to construct a 30 point scale of indicators which distinguish masculine and feminine in the stories of eight- and nine-year-olds. Many of the "feminine" indicators can be found in stories by younger boys, and many of the "masculine" ones in stories by older girls, which may suggest some relationship between conventional femininity and infantilism.

The worst-off appear to be the inner-urban girls, whether Australian or migrant. The settings of their stories are more often restricted to domesticity, and themes include frequent reference to punishment for any deviation or initiative. Girls risk being kidnapped or murdered (and this motive also appears in "disadvantaged" boys' stories about mothers).

Middle-class suburban girls' stories, on the other hand, are often frivolous and trivial, with the main interest in pets or playing games. If tragedy strikes a pet or playmate, the heroine survives unmoved.

Suburban middle-class boys' stories would suggest that they have the greatest psychological advantages, for they have access to the widest range of experiences in both fantasy and realism, in action and feeling, and they have the widest range of vocabulary for their expression.

Appendix II:

LANGUAGE IN STORIES TOLD BY AUSTRALIAN CHILDREN AGED EIGHT TO NINE YEARS

"Restricted codes"

Children's English expression tends to be most limited when they write, according to their physical discomfort in handling the graphic instruments, their degree of impatience, their abilities to sequence, their capacity to put down the word in letters—quite apart from spelling it correctly—and their short-term memory to hold what they intended to say long enough to say it. In all these, the children who told the stories in this book are likely to be deficient.

Their oral language is also likely to be impoverished in public use. The Australian tradition is to be laconic, and although the children may not be aware of this, certainly teenagers at parties and youngsters "talking to the class" seem to have a limited range of expression. It has been documented in research how the "playground English" that migrant children pick up in school is in many localities inadequate to help them learn in classrooms.

The children often seem to be at their most fluent when they are telling their own stories in a private situation. It is then possible to see the degree to which their ideas outrun their capacity to express them. Syntax is often a problem that they are not so aware of, although the listener suffers from the double or even triple negatives, and mixtures of subject and object, as well as the over-use of pronouns unreliably attached to any noun, and the rarity with which characters are given their own names. But the children are often aware of how their limited vocabularies hamper them, and the following lists of "words they wanted" is illuminating about the sort of things eight- and nine-year-olds want to say but cannot.

Inner-suburban children tried to find the words for:

(boys)

> *pilot, on a mission, promotion, ceded, devastation, demoted, satellite, air-marshal, anchor, inflatable, set (the sun), sun shining, rain stopping, demolished, pillar, cell, gunner, turret, stable, fuel, reputation, licence, airport, perspective, tailplane, cabin, accident, investigations, ate up, down the chimney, captured, mate, assault.*

(girls)

crouching, jowls, lost appetite, change their minds, missed opportunity, swims, competing, unsaddle, alone, obey, regular, concluded, choose, travel widely, instigate, permanent, misbehave, fatal, curious, investigate, injured, had magical powers.

Outer suburban children were more rarely at a loss, but needed these:

rodeo, fuel, metal, aluminium, jailed, fare, fillet, offal, unload.

A further distinction between middle-class and working-class children was the latter's tendency to be imprecise about words—the same word quite often had different shapes, and children would not only spell it in different ways in the same sentence, but even give it a variety of pronunciations in the same story e.g.

sunnarine, sunderine, subbarin; umberella, undrel, unnerbrel

In many respects there was no significant difference in the language of story-telling by children of different social class, although there were wide differences between individual children.

No differences were found between average length of stories and complexity of sentences, according to social class (although intelligence is a distinguishing factor—bright children tend to tell longer and more complexly-worded stories). Migrant children understandably made the most errors in grammar and syntax, but average children in all schools made mistakes—much of the error often being that children speak more logically than our idiomatic English warrants.

No differences were found in numbers of nouns and verbs in stories, although there were some differences in the most popular words. Boys tended to use more nouns referring to objects, occupations, places and nature; girls used more abstract nouns and words concerned with food.

The most popular nouns

For girls: mother, father, girl, home, house, name, night

For urban boys: people, man, home, ship, place, plane, men, fights, army, station, airport, bombs, war, sun

For suburban boys: people, things, home, plane, house, school, man, Dad, door, legs, pilot, person, driver

Girls rarely if ever referred to driver, fights, dinosaur, sports, sea, ambulance, fire-brigade—all popular with boys.

Boys rarely referred to lady or flower.

The most significant difference in use of parts of speech was in adjectives: 12 per cent of urban boys used no adjectives in their stories, but neither did 35 per cent of urban migrant boys and 30 per cent of urban Australian boys, while girls always used adjectives. Urban boys tended to indicate size and amount, suburban boys liked positive adjectives, while girls emphasised description, time and attitude.

The most popular adjectives

For girls: little, all, very, big, scared, wrong, inside, few, quiet, great, proper, really, real, lot of, nice, happy

Urban boys: big, good, little, old, new, fast, great, first, second, pretty (as in pretty big)

Suburban boys: good, very, happy, fast, big, hot, lots of, little, new, fastest, better, nice, broken, always, next

Glossary of Terms

Poor:
the family does not have enough money or material goods, according to some standard.

Underprivileged:
someone who does not have the same chances and opportunities as most other people.

Socially disadvantaged:
the family is considered socially inferior, or the children do not have opportunity to learn social behaviour or survival value, or both.

Culturally disadvantaged:
a child lacks the home or social environment to prepare him or her for learning at school, or learns the wrong things, according to the rest of society. *Educationally disadvantaged* may be used in the same or a slightly narrower sense.

Industrial suburb:
contains heavy industry and workers' homes.

Inner suburb:
an old working-class area with high population density close to the city centre.

Working class:
"blue collar workers". On no account to be equated with *deprived, disadvantaged,* etc. as these terms can cut across social class, and particularly involve non-workers.

Middle class:
used here mainly for those who own their own homes in the suburbs, whatever their occupation.

Deprived:
lacks a necessity, socially, culturally, emotionally, or physically, and others are to blame.

Handicapped:
it is harder for the child to do what other children do because he has specific difficulties. Others may not be to blame.

Disadvantaged:
a child has less chance than others of learning how to become the sort of person "we" think he should. It may not be clear whether the problem is basically socio-economic, constitutional, or bad luck.

Maladjusted:
does not fit in with everyone else, which causes trouble for the child and everyone else. This may be the fault of everyone else, and it should

not be assumed that children should become *adjusted*.
Fantasy:
used here for daydreams which children express when asked to tell
stories "off the top of their heads" and which are spun as they are
told.
Normal child:
impossible to define in practice, but in theory the normal healthy
child can learn to love and to work, and to gain satisfaction from
both.
Euphemism:
word used with the aim of offending nobody. Any of the words above
can be used as euphemisms, which helps them to become confused
with each other.
Value judgements:
impossible to avoid in this subject, and the value judgement has been
made that it is safer to try to recognise and identify them, than to
imagine one is being really objective.
Sentiment:
"*The value of sentiment is the amount of sacrifice you are prepared to make for
it.*" Galsworthy.